The Caucasian Chalk Circle

Bertolt Brecht (1898–1956) is acknowledged as one of the great dramatists whose work has had a considerable influence on the theatre. His landmark plays include *Mother Courage and Her Children*, *The Threepenny Opera*, *The Life of Galileo* and *The Caucasian Chalk Circle*. His plays and dramatic theory are central to the study of modern theatre.

Kristopher Imbrigotta is Assistant Professor of German Studies at the University of Puget Sound (Tacoma, USA). His research and teaching cover literature and cultural studies from the late nineteenth and twentieth centuries, focusing primarily on theatre history and drama pedagogy; visual culture and film; memory discourses and literary historiography; and environmental humanities. He is co-editor of the performance journal *Communications of the International Brecht Society* and an elected member of the steering committee for the Brecht Society. He is also a member of the international translation team for the latest edition of *Brecht on Theatre* (2014).

Other Bertolt Brecht publications by Methuen Drama

Brecht Collected Plays: One
(Baal, Drams in the Night, In the Jungle of Cities, The Life of Edward II of England, A Respectable Wedding, The Beggar or the Dead Dog, Driving Out a Devil, Lux in Tenebris, The Catch)

Brecht Collected Plays: Two
(Man Equals Man, The Elephant Calf, The Threepenny Opera, The Rise and Fall of the City of Mahagonny, The Seven Deadly Sins)

Brecht Collected Plays: Three
(Lindbergh's Flight, The Baden-Baden Lesson on Consent, He Said Yes/He Said No, The Decision, The Mother, The Exception and the Rule, The Horations and the Curiatians, St Joan of the Stockyards)

Brecht Collected Plays: Four
(Round Heads and Pointed Heads, Fear and Misery of the Third Reich, Senora Carrar's Rifles, Dansen, How Much Is Your Iron?, The Trial of Lucullus)

Brecht Collected Plays: Five
(Life of Galileo, Mother Courage and Her Children)

Brecht Collected Plays: Six
(The Good Person of Szechwan, The Resistible Rise of Arturo Ui, Mr Puntila and His Man Matti)

Brecht Collected Plays: Seven
(The Visions of Simone Machard, Schweyk in the Second World War, The Caucasian Chalk Circle, The Duchess of Main)

Brecht Collected Plays: Eight
(The Days of the Commune, The Antigone of Sophocles, Turandot or the Whitewashes' Congress)

Berliner Ensemble Adaptations
(The Tutor, Coriolanus, The Trial of Joan of Arc at Rouen 1431, Don Juan, Trumpets and Drums)

Bertolt Brecht Journals, 1934–55

Brecht on Art and Politics

Brecht on Film and Radio

Brecht on Performance

Brecht on Theatre

Brecht in Practice

The Craft of Theatre: Seminars and Discussions in Brechtian Theatre

Brecht, Music and Culture

Brecht in Context

The Theatre of Bertolt Brecht Brecht: A Choice of Evils

Bertolt Brecht: A Literary Life

A Guide to the Plays of Bertolt Brecht

Bertolt Brecht's Refugee Conversations

Brecht and the Writer's Workshop

Collected Short Stories of Bertolt Brecht

The Business Affairs of Mr Julius Caesar

The Caucasian Chalk Circle

Original work entitled

Der kaukasische Kreidekreis

Translated from the German by

JAMES and TANIA STERN with W.H. AUDEN

BERTOLT BRECHT

with commentary and notes by

KRISTOPHER IMBRIGOTTA

Series Editors: Sara Freeman, Jenny Stevens,

Chris Megson and Matthew Nichols

B L O O M S B U R Y

NEW DELHI • LONDON • OXFORD • NEW YORK • SYDNEY

BLOOMSBURY INDIA
Bloomsbury Publishing India Pvt. Ltd
Second Floor, LSC Building No. 4, DDA Complex, Pocket C–6&7,
Vasant Kunj, New Delhi 110070

BLOOMSBURY, Methuen Drama India and the Diana logo are trademarks of
Bloomsbury Publishing Plc

First published in India 2022
The Caucasian Chalk Circle first published in this translation in Great Britain
by Methuen and Co 1960
This revised Student Edition first published by Methuen Drama 2021
Reprinted 2021

Cover design: Charlotte Daniels
Cover image © Thanee Hengpattanapong / Alamy Stock Photo

British Library Cataloguing-in-Publication Data
A catalogue record for this book is available from the British Library.

Library of Congress Cataloging-in-Publication Data
A catalog record for this book is available from the Library of Congress

ISBN: 978-93-54357-36-7
10 9 8 7 6 5 4 3 2

For sale in the Indian subcontinent only

Typeset by RefineCatch Limited, Bungay, Suffolk
Printed and bound in India by Gopsons Papers Pvt. Ltd. Sivakasi

Bloomsbury Publishing Plc makes every effort to ensure that the papers used in the manufacture of our books are natural, recyclable products made from wood grown in well-managed forests. Our manufacturing processes conform to the environmental regulations of the country of origin.

To find out more about our authors and books
visit www.bloomsbury.com and sign up for our newsletters

Contents

Chronology

Brecht's life falls into three distinct phases demarcated by his forced exile from his native Germany during the Hitler years. From 1898–1933 he is in Germany; from 1933–1947 he is in exile in various parts of the world; in 1947 he returns to Europe, first to Switzerland then to Berlin.

Germany

1898 Eugen Berthold Friedrich Brecht born on 10 February at Augsburg where his father was an employee and later director of the Haindl paper mill.

1908 Brecht goes to Augsburg Grammar School (Realgymnasium) where he is an indifferent pupil and a rebel in his quiet way, numbering among his friends Caspar Neher, later his designer. Brecht was almost expelled for taking a dismissive, anti-patriotic line when set an essay with the title 'It is a sweet and honourable thing to die for one's country'.

1917 Brecht enrols as a medical student at Munich University, where he also attends Arthur Kutscher's theatre seminar. He samples the bohemian literary life of the city.

1918 Brecht is conscripted and serves as a medical orderly, though he still lives at home. He writes *Baal,* a rumbustious, even outrageous dramatic tribute to natural drives and anarchic sexuality, and does theatre reviews for the local newspaper, *Augsburger Neueste Nachrichten.*

1919 Brecht writes *Drums in the Night.* He meets the comedian Karl Valentin, the theatre director Erich Engel, and actresses Elisabeth Bergner, Blandine Ebinger, Carola Neher and Marianne Zoff.

1920 Brecht visits Berlin.

1921 Brecht's registration at Munich University is cancelled. An attempt to make himself known in literary circles in Berlin ends with him in hospital suffering from malnutrition. His new friendship with Arnolt Bronnen, the playwright, leads him to change the spelling of his name to Bertolt, or Bert.

1922 Brecht marries Marianne Zoff. He writes *In the Jungle of Cities.*

1923 Brecht's daughter Hannc is born. The activities of Hitler's National Socialists are hotly discussed in Brecht's Munich circle. The first productions of *In the Jungle of Cities* and *Baal* take place in Munich and Leipzig respectively.

1924 Brecht directs Christopher Marlowe's *Edward II* which he and Lion Feuehtwanger had adapted. He was already using certain devices (plot summaries before scenes, white face make-up to indicate fear) to induce critical detachment in actors and audience. He finally settles in Berlin and is taken on as dramaturg (literary adviser) at Max Reinhardt's Deutsches Theater. The actress Helen Weigel bears him a son, Stefan.

1925 Klabund's *The Chalk Circle,* premiered at Frankfurt and Hanover in January, is directed in Berlin in October by Max Reinhardr with Elisabeth Bergner in the female lead.

1926 *Man Equals Man* premiered at Darmstadt and Düsseldorf. *The Elephant Calf,* an accompanying 'interlude for the foyer', parodies the *Chalk Circle* test. Brecht's work on a play (which he never finished) called *Joe Fleischhacker,* which was to deal with the Chicago Wheat Exchange, leads him to the study of Marx as the only adequate method of analysing the workings of capitalism.

1927 Brecht divorces Marianne Zoff. He works with Erwin Piscator, the pioneer of communist political theatre in Germany, on a dramatisation of Hasek's novel *The Good Soldier Schweik.*

1928 *The Threepenny Opera,* music by Kurt Weill, words by Brecht (based on a translation of John Gay's *Beggar's Opera* by Brecht's friend and collaborator Elisabeth Hauptmann), opens at the Theater am Schiffbauerdamm and becomes the hit of the season, Brecht had provocatively transferred bourgeois manners to a Soho criminal setting.

1929 Brecht marries Helene Weigel. *The Baden-Baden Cantata* is staged at the Baden-Baden Music Festival, music by Hindemith.

1930 Brecht's daughter Barbara born. His *Lehrstück* or didactic play, *The Measures Taken*, is given its first performance in Berlin, The communist didactic plays for amateur performance were intended to clarify the ideas of the performers as much as the audience. The first performance of *The Rise and Fall of the City of Mahogonny*, an opera with words by Brecht and music by Kurt Weill causes a riot as the Nazis voice their criticism at Leipzig. In his notes on the opera Brecht tabulates the differences between the traditional *dramatic* (or Aristolelian) and the new *epic* (or non-Aristotelian) theatre at which he is aiming.

1931 Brecht completes *St Joan of the Stockyards*.

1932 Brecht's only film, *Kuhle Wampe*, is held up by the censor. His dramatisation of Maxim Gorky's novel *The Mother* is performed by a left-wing collective in Berlin, music by Hanns Eisler. It demonstrates the development of a worker's mother towards proletarian class-consciousness. Beginning of Brecht's friendship with Margarete Steffin. Brecht studies Marxism under the dissident communist Karl Korsch.

Exile

1933 The Nazis come to power. The night after the German parliament building (the Reichstag) is burnt down, Brecht flees with his family to Prague. He moves to

Vienna, then Zurich, finally settling on the island of Fyn in Denmark. His friendship with Ruth Berlau begins.

1934 Brecht visits London. The themes of flight and exile enter his poetry.

1935 Brecht is stripped of his German citizenship. He visits Moscow and meets the Soviet dramatist Sergei Tretiakov. He attends the International Writers' Conference in Paris. He visits New York to look in on a production of *The Mother*, which does not meet with his approval.

1936 Brecht attends the International Writers' Conference in London. He writes anti-fascist poetry.

1937 Brecht attends the International Writers' Conference in Paris.

1938 Brecht finishes writing *Life of Galileo. Fear and Misery of The Third Reich* is given its first performance in Paris. Brecht makes notes for an 'Odense' *Chalk Circle* which was to be set in Denmark in the eleventh century.

1939 Brecht moves to Stockholm with his family. He finishes writing *Mother Courage and Her Children*.

1940 German forces march into Denmark. In Lidingö Brecht completes *The Augsburg Chalk Circle*, a short story set in the Thirty Years War. Brecht's household moves to Helsinki in Finland where his friendship with the writer Hella Wuolijoki begins.

1941 Brecht completes *Mr Puntila and his Man Matti, The Good Person of Szechwan* and *The Resistable Rise of Arturo Ui*. He writes war poetry and 'Finnish Epigrams'. Leaving Finland Brecht travels through the Soviet Union via Leningrad and Moscow (where Margarete Steffin dies) to Vladivostock and sails to the United States. He arrives in Los Angeles in July and settles with his family in Santa Monica. He makes contact with other exiles (Heinrich Mann, Lion Feuchtwanger and Fritz Lang, the film director) and with the natives (Orson Welles). First performance of *Mother Courage and Her Children* in neutral Switzerland.

1942 Brecht prepares his *Poems in Exile* for publication. He participates in the anti-war, anti-fascist activities of exile groups. He meets Charles Laughton.

1943 The first performances of *The Good Person of Szechwan* and of *Life of Galileo* take place in Zurich.

1944 Brecht becomes a member of the newly formed Council for a Democratic Germany. The Red Army drives the Germans out of the Caucasus. Following a Broadway contract for the play, arranged by the actress Luise Rainer, Brecht writes the first version of *The Caucasian Chalk Circle*, and almost immediately starts reworking it. W.H. Auden works on an English version with his friends James and Tania Stern. Brecht studies Arthur Waley's translations of Chinese poetry.

1945 *Fear and Misery of the Third Reich* is given its first English performance in New York under the title *The Private Life of the Master Race*. Brecht and Charles Laughton complete an English version of *Life of Galileo*.

1946 The first performance of Brecht's adaptation of Webster's *The Duchess of Malfi* takes place in Boston.

1947 Charles Laughton appears in the title role of *Life of Galileo* in Beverly Hills and New York. Brecht appears before the *House Committee on Unamerican Activities* and proves himself a master of ambiguity when cross-examined about his communist sympathies.

Return

1947 Brecht and Helene Weigel go to Zurich, leaving their son Stefan, who is an American citizen, in the United States. He meets Max Frisch, his old friend and designer Caspar Neher, and the playwright Carl Zuckmayer.

1948 Brecht's adaptation of *Antigone of Sophocles* is performed in Chur, Switzerland, and *Mr Puntila and his Man Matti* is given its first performance in Zurich. He publishes the *Little Organum for the Theatre*. Brecht travels to Berlin and starts rehearsals of *Mother Courage* at the Deutsches Theater in the Soviet sector of the city. *The Caucasian Chalk Circle* is first performed in Eric and Maja Bentley's English translation by students at Northfield, Minnesota.

1949 *Mother Courage* opens at the Deutsches Theater with Helene Weigel in the title role. Brecht visits Zurich again before settling in Berlin. The Berliner Ensemble, Brecht and Weigel's own state-subsidised company, is formed and opens with *Puntila*. The second version of *The Caucasian Chalk Circle* is published in East Berlin by the literary magazine *Sinn und Form*. Brecht applies for an Austrian passport (Weigel is Austrian).

1951 *The Mother* is performed by the Berliner Ensemble. Brecht finishes the first version of his adaptation of Shakespeare's *Coriolanus*.

1953 Brecht is elected President of this German section of the PEN Club, the international writers' association. On 17 June there are strikes and demonstrations protesting about working conditions in the German Democratic Republic. Brecht writes a letter to the Secretary of the Socialist Unity Party which is released to the press in a doctored form.

1954 The Berliner Ensemble moves into its own home, the Theater am Schiffbauerdamm (where he had triumphed with *The Threepenny Opera* in 1928), and performs *The Caucasian Chalk Circle*. The prologue, *The Struggle for the Valley*, is now designated as Act I. Brecht makes public his objections to the Paris Treaty (which incorporated the Federal Republic of Germany into Nato) and to re-armament in general. The Berliner Ensemble's productions of *Mother Courage* and Kleist's *The Broken*

Pitcher are enthusiastically received as the highlights of the Paris Théâtre des Nations festival. *Mother Courage* is awarded the prizes for best play and best production.

1955 Harry Buckwitz, directing the West German premiere of *The Caucasian Chalk Circle* at Frankfurt, omits *The Struggle for the Valley* as politically inopportune.

1956 Brecht is preparing the Berliner Ensemble, which by that time has become generally recognised as the foremost progressive theatre in Europe, for a visit to London when he dies of a heart attack on 14 August. The visit went ahead and *Mother Courage, The Caucasian Chalk Circle* and *Trumpets and Drums* were presented at the Palace Theatre at the end of August for a short season – a landmark in Brecht's reception in the United Kingdom.

Brecht and the Epic Theatre

Epic vs. dramatic

Brecht's dramatic theory is practical, although at first glance it can seem technical and complicated. He wanted to create entertaining *and* politically instructive theatre. All the gestures and devices which we know as 'Brechtian' are experimental efforts to transform how audiences respond to a staged narrative in order to influence and change interpretations of the world, and so – ultimately – to change the world itself. As the chorus of one of his learning plays, *The Decision* (1930), chants, 'Change the world, it needs it!'

Brecht's experiments and eventual theoretical framework for a new type of theatrical presentation evolved over decades into what would become the 'epic theatre.' This is a theatre that introduces a narrative voice into the stage performance. For Brecht, theatre was not supposed to be an enactment that we happen to witness; rather, we should realize that stories are told from a point of view and for a purpose. The experimental position of trying out this or that argument and soliciting the audience's critical response and action became important for Brecht and a hallmark of his dramatic and theatrical practice, which sought to engage the public, not just emotionally, but also intellectually.

This narration on stage directly interfaces with the audience and breaks the barriers created between actor and spectator. The overt mediation of the story, Brecht believed, was bound to provoke more reflection in his spectators. What they see is no longer a straightforward imitation of a real action, in which they become emotionally involved to the exclusion of all other responses; it is rather a story they are being told and upon which they are invited to reflect critically: Could it have happened differently? How did we get here? These are questions which are often explicitly broached within Brecht's plays. It is a reflection of Brecht's own attitude toward art in general – not a mirror that reflects reality, but rather a hammer with which to smash our perceptions.

From the ancient Greek writer Aristotle, Brecht learned about the classical 'dramatic' model of theatre with its traditional three unities of time (the action occurs in one day), place (the action occurs in one single location or setting) and action (one principle theme). For Aristotle, the dramatic form (specifically tragedy) aimed for purging, or *catharsis*, of the audience's emotions through empathy and identification with the characters. Brecht proposed replacing empathy with knowledge and reason. The audience could get involved and be moved by the dramatic action – many of Brecht's characters are witty, humorous, and pitiful – but they were not to empathize to such an extent that they could envision no alternatives. Already in his play *Drums in the Night* (1920), Brecht had begun to signal these intentions with placards on stage that read provocatively: 'Don't stare so romantically!' This is not only an attack on the established theatre institution but also a direct challenge for contemporary theatre-goers to become critical observers and re-learn how to understand artistic messages in the service of social change. Aristotelian tragedy, he thought, brought about a passivity that could only serve political conformism, not something conducive to active participation in shaping society or fomenting change. Brecht wanted to create a pedagogic theatre that could help cultivate an informed and questioning public. We are supposed to come out of the epic theatre thinking: That was terrible, but why is life really like that? We have seen one response to a situation, but was it the necessary response? How could we envisage a different outcome?

These questions highlight clearly that Brecht's epic theatre is not opposed to emotion or identification. On the contrary, emotional sympathy often motivates progress and action. An excess of emotion, or the indulgence of emotion to the exclusion of intelligent reflection, is what Brecht wanted us to avoid. Brecht's epic theatre shows humans as socially constructed and struggling with the great forces of the day. These, rather than the inner lives of individuals, become the subject matter and causalities of the new 'epic theatre', whose analysis justifies Brecht's later proclamation of a 'theatre for the scientific age'.

One can readily find epic techniques in *The Caucasian Chalk Circle*. Beginning in the Prologue, for example, as the two kolchos farmer groups decide to listen and perform the parable play of the 'Chalk Circle' we are introduced to the Singer. His first lines tell the audience about what they are about to observe: a play with songs, using the 'old masks' where the 'whole kolchos takes part' (34). Here, the Singer points out explicitly that we are about to witness a play (even though the play has already begun) and that we as critical observers should pay close attention to the action because it has important parallels and implications for the present day. The Expert, perhaps to be understood as a direct interjection from Brecht himself into the play, has a short exchange with the Singer (34–5). From there, we enter the narrative world of the revolution in Grusinia that will lead us to the eventual parable of the 'Chalk Circle' at the end of the play in Scene 6. In this short exchange, the Expert (Brecht?) poses flippant questions that are perhaps on the minds of the kolchos farmers in the play, but also of the spectators in the audience: How long will the performance last? Does it have to be this long? The Singer replies to our questions and sets up the expectations that the play requires of us: there will be multiple stories requiring our attention, and no, it cannot be any other way. The take away here illustrates what the epic actor seeks to accomplish: we remain aware that we are watching a play, we must prepare ourselves to observe and analyze the upcoming events, and we should do all this with an eye on our contemporary social situations.

Verfremdungseffekt, or the process of making strange

Of all the dramatic theories Brecht developed, this was at the time one of the most important, and it has since become the hallmark that defines epic theatre. In 1939 Brecht wrote: 'To subject an event or character to *Verfremdung* means, first of all, divesting the event or character of everything self-evident, familiar and apparently obvious and, instead, provoking astonishment and curiosity about them. [. . .] *Verfremdung* thus implies historicization, it means representing events and people as historical. Of course you can do the same thing with contemporaries, their attitudes too can be presented as 'of their time', historical, transitory.'[1] Astonishment and curiosity are not

1 'On Experimental Theatre'. *Brecht on Theatre*. Eds. Steve Giles, Tom Kuhn and Marc Silberman, trans. Silberman. London: Bloomsbury, 2014. 133–5, here 143–4.

enough. It is no longer just a question of separating the experience of the audience (and the actors) from that of the theatrical characters; rather, it is an attempt to make productive that awareness of surprise, dismay or discomfort which follows from jolting the audience's unexamined assumptions about their history, about society, and art. It is not merely exposing the artistic device of the theatre self-consciously revealing its own tricks; rather, *Verfremdung* amounts to seeing through the customs, habits and positions that constitute ideology (i.e., a system or set of beliefs for a person or group).

Verfremdung is the concept for the mobilization of the effects which we know as Brechtian and which help to deliver epic theatre, including the devices assuring that we can never identify too completely with the characters, never get emotionally swept up by the action, and always come to critical analysis. These may be purely textual – the historically or geographically remote settings, the songs – but they also include aspects of production and acting technique discussed below and that reside in the play text and on stage that remind us we are in the theatre: direct address of the audience, emblematic props, the use of projected commentaries and placards, masks, music, and an acting style which was meant to reveal what it is that structures the socialized human being.

Concept and Context

Inception of the play

Brecht used essentially two main sources for writing *The Caucasian Chalk Circle*. The earliest inspiration can be traced back approximately to 1924, as Brecht read Klabund's (Alfred Henschke) German-language translation of the Chinese play *The Chalk Circle*. Here, the emperor's main wife tries to claim maternal rights to another woman's child. A wise judge orders both women to pull the arms of the child within a circle drawn in chalk, with the true mother to be revealed as the one who can pull him across the line. The biological mother, seeking to protect her child, releases him. The judge therefore recognizes her as the true mother. Brecht was also familiar with the biblical parable of King Solomon (1 Kings 3.16–28). In this story, the king must decide on a similar case of motherhood and, instead of a tug-of-war within the circle, proposes something more violent: to cut the child in two using a sword. Solomon's line of thinking is similar to the judge in the Chinese story: the true mother will act to protect her child and would rather relent than see it harmed or killed. Aside from this central theme, all other elements in Brecht's play are his own.

Brecht worked on *The Caucasian Chalk Circle* mainly during his exile years starting around 1944, work that he carried with him from Europe to the United States and culminated in two major versions (1949 and 1953/4) with revisions to the original story. While in Sweden, Brecht wrote a short story called 'The Augsburg Chalk Circle' which contained most of the storyline for the eventual play, complete with the fleeing child, the adoption, and the judgment in court. The short story, however, was historically set in seventeenth-century central Europe during the Thirty Years' War.[2] In 1944, while living in southern California, Brecht finished much of the first version of the play, deciding on the Caucasus region that borders southeastern Europe and western Asia for its setting.

2 The Thirty Years' War also plays a major role as historical setting in Brecht's play *Mother Courage*.

The play takes place in Grusinia, a Russian variant for Georgia, then a Soviet satellite state in the Eastern Bloc. Soviet Georgia as backdrop for the play was significant, with Brecht having expressed an early optimism in communism. It also fuelled his decision to return from exile and enter the German Democratic Republic (GDR, former East Germany) in 1948. Brecht viewed the socialist politics and rhetoric from the Soviet Union and the GDR as a potential positive force in the reconstruction of a defeated Germany after the Second World War. In the play, this is manifest in the State Reconstruction Commission in the opening Prologue. His hopes for a better postwar Germany eventually diminished as the brutal realities of the socialist regime in the GDR became apparent. The play had its premiere in a small university town in the United States (Carleton College in Northfield, Minnesota) to an English-speaking audience using Eric Bentley's translation, not on the German stage. After the 1953/4 revisions Brecht had his longtime musical collaborator, Paul Dessau, compose music for it. The play was performed for the first time in German with the Berliner Ensemble at the Theater am Schiffbauerdamm (Brecht's own company and theatre house) in East Berlin.

Nationalism and nation after the Second World War

As with many of Brecht's works first written in exile, revised and eventually staged in the GDR, *The Caucasian Chalk Circle* should be understood within the historical context of the fall of Nazi Germany and its aftermath. 'Denazification', the process of dismantling National Socialist ideology and decoupling it from German culture, politics, media and press, the legal system and the economy, had begun in the British, American and French Occupation Zones of western and southern Germany as soon as late 1945. The GDR lay within the Soviet Occupation Zone and therefore allied with the Soviet Union after becoming a state in 1949. Financial assistance in the form of a massive economic recovery plan for the Federal Republic of Germany (FRG, former West Germany) from the American government known as the Marshall Plan served two purposes: it not only promised to help rebuild the FRG from the ruins of war, but also to garner favour with West German civilians in desperate need of aid. If Germans, especially in the west, would turn to America and capitalism, it would dissuade them from looking east toward the growing superpower of the Soviet Union and communism. This, of course, was the pretext for the GDR government erecting the Berlin Wall in 1961 that geographically and ideologically separated East and West.

The events in this play also mirror Brecht's own exile experience: he and his family fled Germany immediately after the Nazis took power in 1933 and they were effectively stateless as they moved across Europe and Asia, and eventually settled in southern California among other German émigrés. Brecht had no place to stage his German-language plays. In Scene 4, Grusha has the same problems as she seeks help from her brother, Lavrenti (77); or, for example, in the Prologue from the Expert about nation, 'loving one's country', and problems of identity (30–1).

The group of villagers and officials are talking about belonging and the complex nature of national identity. Here, Brecht reminds us that such notions are complicated during times of war and upheaval, but also contradictory. While it is a basic (and encouraged) tenet of democratic societies to criticize one's own homeland when physically present in that space, it is another thing entirely once you are either removed from it or it is erased from the map; in that case, as we see above, the importance of place is nothing to be taken for granted, and indeed, something one longs for if absent.

We find many reference points to these historical events in the play. In the Prologue, the word 'Nazi' appears in the very first line of dialogue. In Scene 3, Grusha's attempt at crossing the bridge on her way into the mountains is a metaphor for the struggle in postwar Germany (68–70). Also on a macro level in Scene 2, the Stableman talks to other servants as the Governor's household prepares to flee: 'This is going to be an unhealthy place for some time' (49). His remarks about the rebuilding of everyday life in Grusinia echo that of German life in the late 1940s.

Narrative Structure

A play about a play within a play: Episodes

The Caucasian Chalk Circle is a play within a play – a parable about social systems, the hardships of war and the power of motherhood. Its first scene, or Prologue, in which workers from two Soviet kolchos farmer collectives gather to discuss land reform after the Second World War, is an external frame meant to bookend the plot, or at least introduce it, to a contemporary audience. However, Brecht further complicates this setup because the play never formally returns to or ends with the kolchos setting in the Caucasus, with the exception of perhaps the very last lines from the Singer in Scene 6. Practically speaking, we may even lose that narrative thread by the final scene, not only because the story never returns to the 'struggle for the valley' but also because after the Prologue we become interested in the fates of Grusha, Michael and then Azdak. In fact, following the circular and episodic structure of this play, one might even argue that there are essentially two plays going on within the outer frame of the kolchos storyline: one of Grusha and her struggle to flee civil war and fight for Michael, and another tale of the unlikely judge Azdak who dispenses proper 'justice' in all the wrong ways (more on Azdak and why he is such a distinctly Brechtian invention below).

In Scenes 2–4, the audience follows Grusha through various stations in Grusinia over a period of several years. It is then further explained at the start of Scene 5 that two years have passed, as we circle back two years prior to the revolution in Scene 2. Scene 5 proceeds to tell the backstory of Azdak – seemingly unrelated at first to Grusha and her plight, but related to the circumstances surrounding the disappearance of the Grand Duke after he must flee. In the final scene, Grusha's trial subsequently links the Grusha and Azdak narratives for the moral of the story, until that point parallel but separate tales. Grusha prevails and is awarded Michael. If this seems convoluted, it probably is but with purpose.

Brecht's preference for the episodic does not hinder him from paying close attention to plot structure; in fact, it is just the opposite. The episodic, somewhat back-and-forth nature of Brecht's plays serve to highlight the very fact that we are sitting in the theatre observing actions on a stage. His plays and characters are neither natural nor realistic, but seek to show the audience how and why any given action is taking place vis-à-vis social structures, political realities, and historical forces. Brecht's plays are not one thing after the other: first A, then B, and finally C. Rather, Brecht often employs such techniques that disturb our linear thinking and the act of storytelling in order to make us aware of important points, sometimes in overt ways, but often without explicit dialogue or direction from the actors. This, in tandem with other epic techniques, points the audience in multiple directions. Scene 6, for example, is prepared carefully on stage with Azdak's previous verdicts in mind from Scene 5. Not only are the decisions quite random and rendered in humorous ways; they are also purposeful. They come to define Azdak's motives and the play's circular structure. The divorce case for the old couple in that scene illustrates this nicely. On the surface, the situation seems silly and irrelevant on stage, perhaps a bit of comedic flourish to draw out the suspense, only until we realize that Brecht introduces it intentionally to set up the harmonious resolution at the end of the play.

The circle motif

The play opens with members of two kolchos farmer collectives sitting in a circle, smoking and drinking wine as they begin to discuss the new plans from the Reconstruction Commission. This is the very first image that the audience sees. Grusha, in another example, flees with the child to escape the fighting in Grusinia in Scenes 2 and 3 but by the end of the play she has returned to Grusinia to face the question of her parental rights against Michael's biological mother. Her return home sets up much of the main action for the entire play and culminates in the climax where an actual circle is drawn as a 'wrestling ring'. Likewise, the Grand Duke is another character that flees and eventually returns to lead the counterattack against the revolution. Simon Chachava, the soldier who professes his affection for Grusha in Scene 2 amidst the chaos of the fighting, returns to Grusha's side by the river in Scene 4 and realizes there is now a child in Grusha's life, making any hopes of love and a relationship between them seem impossible. Simon is too late in his return and must turn away in despair.

Apart from the play's structure, there is also an element of rhetorical repetition found at various points in the dialogue. For example: in Scene 3, Grusha tries to buy milk for Michael from the Old Man on her way into the northern mountains. Before she finds his home, she sings a song about the 'Four Generals' (53–4) that consists exclusively of repeating lines, or lines that relate to the next with the slightest of variation. After meeting the Old Man, Grusha asks to buy milk and a corn cake for Michael only to be rebuffed multiple times in a similar fashion: the denial of Grusha's wishes happens again and again with minor variations, and is constant throughout the play until the very end as she wins the right to keep Michael. The Old Man finally agrees, but only after Grusha pays an exorbitant amount of money, a 'cutthroat price'. The Old Man's haggling also exhibits this rhetorical flourish of slight variation, repeating his sentiments that if Grusha wants milk she must either 'go to the soldiers' (for they have taken his goats) or subsequently 'kill the soldiers'. In the same vein, the Singer has a tendency to repeat himself, and circle back on major themes in his songs. For example, as the play within the play begins in Scene 2, the Singer leafs through his 'script' and introduces the audience to the dire situation in Grusinia, caused by Governor Abashvili. In this song, the Singer repeats 'Once upon a time' five times, a line that one finds at the beginning of many fairy tales in the folk tradition (35–6). Such repetitions, returning and circular motifs call attention to important dialogue and action and require us as observers to focus closely and interrogate the function and sequence of that moment on stage.

Brecht's epic narrator: The Singer and the song

The Singer, Arkadi Chiedze, best exemplifies Brecht's penchant for combining storytelling and theatrical performance. Scenes in the play are mixed with songs, mostly in the form of passages by the Singer. This character intentionally stands apart from the others: he does not take part directly in any action; rather, as an example of *Verfremdung*, he is there for us, to direct our attention, point to important moments and actions, introduce and review what we will or have already seen, and present the play through a critical lens. Song is important for the epic theatre since it interrupts the action and reminds us that we are observing a play. And, for Brecht, art is not a mirror of reality but an imaginary medium with which we can expose and change things. In *The Caucasian Chalk Circle*, as with many of his other plays, Brecht employs music and song to provide brief commentary and context – mostly for the audience but also, in another nod to the 'epic' in epic theatre, to his actors on stage during the play. The songs, in all approximately forty, vary in purpose and effect. The Singer delivers most, although he is sometimes joined by the Chorus, with the occasional song by other characters (Grusha, the Ironshirts and Azdak). Because the songs essentially lie outside the realm of the dialogue in the play, we must therefore pay extra attention to their message and fully appreciate their function; they are a major element of the play. With the exception of the Prologue and the end of Scene 4, every scene opens and finishes with a song.

The Singer is the most important musical performer on stage, both in his role as storyteller (narrator) and commentator. He is significant as a breaker of illusions, normally associated with the 'dramatic' form of theatre, that seek to show reality. The Singer sings for us on stage, and in doing so, breaks through the illusionist 'fourth wall' – the perceived barrier between the audience and the actors. Notice how the Singer addresses the audience directly; this interrupts the actions and sequence on stage and reminds us that we are watching a play. Most often this happens when the Singer begins a certain song that points to or poses a question about past, present, and future actions. He breaks through to us at the beginning of Scenes 5 and 6. Scene 5 begins with: 'Listen now to the story of the Judge: how he turned Judge, how he passed judgment, what kind of Judge he is' (91). Scene 6 commences thus: 'Now listen to the story of the trial concerning the child of the Governor

Abashvili to establish the true mother by the famous test of the Chalk Circle' (114). The Singer models the role of observer for the audience but also is our 'stand in' and represents us within the play. He sets the stage for subsequent scenes, introduces characters and comments.

Social Relations, Class and Justice

Socialization and socialism: The Prologue

The Prologue, often called the 'socialist' envelope that wraps the play's inner storylines, begins with two Soviet-style kolchos farmer collectives meeting to discuss plans for reconstruction. This socialist frame provides the context for the rest of the play – not only for the Prologue itself, but also throughout episodes in each of the subsequent scenes. Brecht included the Prologue to the original play at a later point after 1944, and it reflects not only his political, social and ideological leanings, but also those in the Soviet zone of eastern Germany who wished to build a socialist state after the fall of Nazism in Europe. This context is important for our understanding of the social behaviours we see in the play.

The Prologue is illustrative of what was going on in Eastern Europe at the time. For example, we see the very language of socialism employed with the 'Rosa Luxemburg' and Galinsk kolchos farmers, and all the characters referring to each other as 'comrade'. The state, represented by experts from the Reconstruction Commission and delegates from the capital, asserts its central authority over economic activity and land reform, the process of expropriation and redistribution of land and wealth. Land reform would have resonated strongly with a contemporary audience in the mid-1950s GDR, as the government policy known as the 'New Course' (German: *Neuer Kurs*) gained traction and was eventually implemented in June 1956.[3] The realm of culture was also seen within the purview of the state authorities having a vested interest in the promotion (production) of the arts, as seen in the Prologue as the Old Man says to the Expert from the state commission: 'You arrange the new distribution of grapevines and tractors. Why not of songs, too?' (34). A distinct 'Socialist Realism' was developed and then sanctioned by the Soviet Union and its satellite countries to show the worker and farmer in real life situations as a hero of socialist society and its

[3] See also Brecht's play *Katzgraben* about a farming village in the GDR dealing with the effects of the 'New Course'.

primary source of power (at least in theory). In the Prologue, the characters gathered at the kolchos meeting follow this progressive ideal and are even the ones who will be performing the play – for the workers by the workers, sung by the Singer. The characters include a Wounded Soldier, an Expert from the planning commission, Farmer, Peasant, an Agronomist, and even a Girl Tractor Driver. Both China and the Soviet Union, allied with the GDR, figure prominently and are used as models: the Singer mentions the Chinese origins of the folk tale 'The Chalk Circle' and celebrates the mixing of both the native and Soviet culture in the play. The play about to be performed signals hope for a future of progressive cooperation: 'We hope you find that the voice of the old poet also sounds well in the shadow of Soviet tractors. It may be mistaken to mix different wines, but old and new wisdom mix very well' (8).

Social inequality

In much of his work, including this play, Brecht examines notions of class, social relations and the abuses of power in the capitalist system. The play exhibits a strong political impulse toward social class and class difference and seeks to expose the underlying social inequalities. To understand class and social structure, we must also examine how socialization informs the actions and worldview of the characters in the play. Socialization briefly defined is the process in which an individual internalizes the norms and ideologies within one's culture and society. Within the context of his work, Brecht sought to re-condition his audience in order to critically observe language and behavior patterns in the theatre and to scrutinize the historical and cultural factors that affect us. In addition to the audience, Brecht sought to re-function the 'behaviour' (or method) of his actors in the epic theatre as well, with the goal of making these forces of socialization on stage both visible and recognizable. However, Brecht did believe that change is possible and, indeed, a necessary imperative in order for culture and society to progress and improve, particularly for the working class.

Brecht was a materialist and self-described Marxist, having studied the social and economic theories by the German writer Karl

Marx (1818–1883). He believed that ideas and actions originate from concrete social conditions that are set by historical factors and attempted to show this causality in his plays. The exchange of service and money is key to showing this on stage, and in doing so, Brecht invites his audience to think about the underlying root causes and outcomes of such transactions: why and for whom (who benefits)? In that sense, characters are not just exchanging money or goods, but showing – not always telling – the rather complex nexus of themes and concepts that reveal how our social systems function. The play has many examples of this, such as the episode in Scene 2 already described above where Grusha tries to buy milk from the Old Man. From a different 'materialist' perspective, one might characterize the actions as extortion by the Old Man as he tries to exploit Grusha's love for Michael and her need to feed him (54–5). Brecht's stage directions – not necessarily the dialogue – are extremely important for this exchange between Grusha and the Old Man. This is the pivotal moment on stage where Grusha can show us these underlying causes for the dominant social structure. She 'rummages' around in her money purse for coins and, by taking her time fishing out what she needs, her actions carry significant meaning visually in two crucial ways: first, she can stall and use this time to show us that she is assessing her dire situation as we should be, namely that that she has no money and cannot afford such a price for the milk; second, we realize that she has no money and she is forced to make a decision that will not benefit her. As a critical audience, Brecht wants us to stop and ponder why Grusha spends her only piasters on Michael. She 'rummages a long time' not because she cannot find the coins, but because she does not have any and this fact must be shown; her decision will alter her situation.

The Prologue presents us directly with themes of social class and a new social order. The storylines which take place in Grusinia with Grusha fighting for custody of Michael, and of how Azdak becomes the judge, seem to be a sort of fairy tale about social justice – the relative happy end for those who suffer but act morally, and the just punishment of those who are bad and immoral. Other fairy tale elements in the play that require the suspension of reality include Grusha's daring escape from the Ironshirts; her treacherous yet miraculous crossing of the bridge into the mountains; the 'dead' husband, whom Grusha has promised to marry for her security, makes a seemingly impossible recovery; the last-minute, almost random reappointment of Azdak as the judge; and the reversed dichotomy between Grusha as the child's good caretaker-stepmother and the Governor's Wife, Natella Abashvili, who is the malevolent mother.

Grusinia is a place rife with social unrest due to the stark differences between the characters' classes. The play takes us back to the Thirty Years' War to a place modelled after a feudal system that exploits the underclass for their labour and must obey the upper-class elites who profit from and rely on that very exploitation as the basis for their wealth and power. The elites in Grusinia exhibit all these negative qualities. For example, Governor Abashvili uses his office to maintain the rigid social hierarchy between the powerful and powerless, allowing him to preserve and enhance his personal life of luxury. The Ironshirts, in turn, are paid to keep the status quo and therefore also profit from the preservation and perpetuation of this system of oppression and exploitation; from a Brechtian stance this is ironic because the soldiers are also from the underclass and act against their own interests for the promise of money. The Governor actually does very little governing: he has no concern for the oppression of the people, for how Grusinia is run, nor does he particularly care how his soldiers deal with the uprising against his government, ultimately leading to his downfall. The Governor's Wife shares her husband's penchant for greed, excess and pure individual interest. In Scene 2 we get a sense of her priorities: her dresses mean more to her than her son. She cannot decide which material goods she will take with her as she flees, and in the tumult forgets to notice that her child is not with her. She is the character whose actions and speech exhibit the most overt disdain for the masses, saying during one exchange in Scene 6: 'I can't stand their smell. It gives me a migraine' (116, also 47 and 59). The Fat Prince, too, is merely interested in power, not reforming the social order that places him at the top of the system. In Scene 2, he suggests that doctors should be punished if people fall ill (37).

Many sympathetic figures in this play hail from the lower-class peasantry. These characters are virtuous and portrayed positively for the most part. Grusha and Simon, for example, have minor flaws, one being their lack of attention to their own well-being: Grusha sacrifices herself for Michael because she cares for him and it is the right thing to do; and Simon, whose love for Grusha goes against his own self-interest and is the cause of his eventual unhappiness. In Scene 2, as Grusha flees with the child and also grows increasingly attached to him, the Singer interjects 'loudly': 'Terrible is the temptation to do good!' underscoring, through an act of *Verfremdung*, the very thought that she is acting against her own interest even though we understand why (52). Azdak, although hailing from the lower class, is raised up by the Fat Prince into a higher social group. He is a unique character in that he presents us with traits from both the upper and lower social groups: on the one hand in his position of authority, he has a penchant for money and corruption that influences his decisions, but at the same time he recognizes that his roots are with the common people and even though his judgements may not conform to typical legal standards (he often makes them up as he goes along), he arrives at them with social justice at heart.

As noted above, the minor characters from the peasantry help to illustrate Brecht's views on social justice. Although many go against their own class and social groups, and are less appealing characters on stage, we must see them as products of the system of oppression in Grusinia. They are greedy, conniving and selfish because they act from their positions of poverty; here, Brecht emphasizes that these characters cannot help the fact that they are this way. Such a perspective does not justify the behaviour, but Brecht asks his audience to, at the very least, acknowledge this fact. We see how false and unproductive the notion is that to rise above one's station in life one must step on those around them, essentially emulating the gross and immoral actions of those in higher positions of authority. Many of the minor characters from the peasantry and lower classes in *The Caucasian Chalk Circle* turn on one another either to please those in power or in an attempt to make personal gain. The irony of course is that these characters will betray their class without ever being able to achieve their end-goals. Essentially, Brecht shows us how the lack of solidarity among those in the same social class not only harms those individuals but also the entire group itself.

One example is in Scene 2, as the servants to the Governor's Wife bustle about gathering her possessions as the palace prepares to depart because of the insurgence. One servant after another – the Cook, Chef, Stableman and Nurse – overlooks the child. Grusha quite typically is present and gets naively caught up in the urgent drama of who will take the child. The Nurse is attuned to this apparent weakness in Grusha and proceeds to act in self-preservation; she doesn't want the child, for if she is caught with him she will be killed like the rest of the Governor's family (49). Once again, Brecht's stage directions (e.g. '*deceitfully*') make all the difference in this sequence. The Nurse knows what will happen to the child and saves herself by sacrificing someone else. Grusha does what is right and realizes quickly that the child is now her burden and she must protect it, even against the advice of the other servants. After this moment, Grusha realizes that she has been fooled by one of her own.

In Scene 3, Grusha seeks shelter for her and the child at an inn among a group of other women who are above her class. Grusha tries unsuccessfully to pass as one of them and is exposed not by her lies but by her body, for the other women see clearly that Grusha's coarse hands mark her as a servant, not a lady. As the ladies force her and Michael to leave the inn, the servant woman chides Grusha for being so naïve to think that she could impersonate a lady above her own class (59–60). Later in Scene 3, as Grusha and the child come upon a house and hope to hide from the Ironshirts chasing them, the Peasant Woman first offers them protection. However, at the first hint of a threat from the soldiers the Peasant Woman betrays Grusha without a second thought in an act of self-preservation, not out of malice but fear.

Law, truth and (in)equity

The play confronts the audience immediately with themes of truth, justice and efficacy in contemporary social systems, as the Old Man says in the Prologue: 'Cheese is not cheese because grass is not grass' (30). Here we get to the pith of Brecht's message: behind the façade of normalcy, nothing is really what it seems. The underlying social structures that were in place have drastically shifted the perception of reality and truth. In a different example of the shifting of social truths from Scene 4, Grusha arrives at her brother's home seeking refuge. Lavrenti concocts a plan to protect Grusha and hide Michael by arranging and paying for a fake marriage to a dying man from the next village, Yussup. Seeing no other alternative, Grusha consents, going against her better judgment to save Michael, and becomes a victim of her own morality: 'Now I'm the fool' she says (77). Lavrenti's marriage scheme hints at the lack of agency that Grusha has in these decisions involving her, and ultimately exposes how discriminatory the social institution of marriage is, here truly based on monetary transaction and legal contracts rather than love. Lavrenti pays a monk rather than a priest because a monk is cheaper and thus mocks religion itself as a business. In fact, the bargain ceremony is supposed to double as a funeral for Yussup who is lying on his deathbed, as we see from the Monk: 'Dear wedding guests and mourners!' (81)

The play employs the backdrop of war (both the Second World War in the Prologue and the peasant revolt against the regime in Grusinia) to highlight issues within the dialectics of justice and the law. We must question our deepest held assumptions about what war actually is and what it means to 'win'. Who benefits – those who profit from it, not those who execute it. Such fundamental interrogation of the social status quo in the play comes mainly from Azdak and is reinforced by the Singer. Azdak's main purpose is to upset those social norms for the audience so that we may challenge our own beliefs and truths. From him we learn that war is good business but brings no justice whereas peace costs money for those in power (96–7). Indeed, the irony of war is that, although it may lead to social change, it inevitably comes at a heavy price for those who can least afford to pay.

The character of Azdak, as stated above, deserves specific attention, particularly in the realm of truth and justice. He is a very Brechtian figure because he is two-sided and contradictory, even lamenting the reversal of the social order that his judgments brought about (112). With a sharp wit and flair for humour, he shows us the cracks in the system of priviledge and lays bare the contradictions that support those systemic inequities. As we learn in Scene 5, he is chosen as judge by the Ironshirts and later unwittingly helps the disguised Grand Duke who is escaping the turmoil of the uprising;

his reward is the reappointment as judge to the consternation of the Governor's Wife. Azdak is extraordinary because nothing about his appearance, behaviour, or language is what it seems on the surface and therefore we must look deeper. Holding his 'court' in taverns, he is often drunk and crass, but this makes him more truthful (not unlike Brecht's Puntila). He scoffs at the upper class and elites but he uses their system of rules against them. He is not necessarily a man of intellect but of feelings and instinct, which help him to deliver his unorthodox judgments. He is unafraid to abuse his position and openly benefits from it by accepting bribes, opening proceedings with 'I receive' and his hand out to collect. He asks defendants: 'You want justice but do you want to pay for it?' (122). Azdak subverts the allegory of the blind woman of justice in the name of perverted transparency – with the right payment, anyone can 'dispose of the formalities' in the legal system and buy the preferred outcome (106). Azdak's real power as a character lies in his rhetoric and skill in asking the 'wrong' questions to greatest effect – wrong in the eyes of the law, but morally just – going against the grain of what is expected within the law.

The system that allows a flawed man like Azdak to sit in judgement over others is the very same one that is exposed as rotten to the core. His decisions are based on whim and corruption, the very things that the legal system only pretends to fight, and present the illusion of justice, which in this play is more powerful than the real thing. In Scene 5, we witness his decision-making first hand: first, the Doctor is found innocent even though he caused his patient's injury; in Azdak's view, he is guilty of malpractice only because he cannot help the fact of being a horrible medical practitioner – essentially guilty of the wrong crime and therefore unpunishable (105). In a different judgment against the farmers concerning the theft of their cow by a Robin Hood-like bandit, Azdak rules in favour of the Old Woman who received the bandit's plunder. The situation 'strikes straight at the court's heart' (110); the audience must ask: Couldn't the law be different and fairer for those in need? Azdak twists the law and does not consider it a crime to receive a cow or a ham if it is something that one needs in order to survive. In the end, he dismisses the farmers' claims even though they are legitimate. The Old Woman was indeed in possession of stolen property but according to Azdak's justice she deserved those things, regardless of how she got them. Azdak's final decision in the play to grant Grusha custody of the child is also the right one, even though it goes against what is lawful. His decision in favour of Grusha is the ultimate act of this type of justice – narrated by the Singer: 'that what there is shall belong to those who are good for it' (128).

For Azdak, it is moral to break a law that is not just because it amplifies the injustice embedded in the system. Here, we realize that Azdak, a flawed and perhaps immoral man, is truly the best person to dispense justice in a system that is unjust. Brecht uses this turn of logic to make his point: Azdak is the right choice precisely because he is not the right person to uphold the current corrupt system. Law and order does not equate to justice; the law is a cold, unequal and subjective process – Azdak lays this out on stage and it is explicitly announced by other characters, such as the Cook to Grusha at the start of her trial: 'This is not a real Judge; this is Azdak. He's a drunk and doesn't understand anything. And the biggest thieves have been acquitted by him, because he mixes everything up and because the rich never offer him big enough bribes' (114). Brecht ultimately reminds us that we have a system of laws not a system of justice and that, unlike Azdak, we are asking the wrong questions.

Motherhood

Asking the right questions is central to the concept of motherhood in the play. Indeed, Brecht uses this theme to interrogate and unsettle its meaning in order to question the social contract of responsibility. While the Governor's Wife is the child's undisputed biological parent, Grusha has been the only mother figure he has known. Her motherliness develops out of her sense of obligation and moral compass. The Singer narrates Grusha's inner thoughts on maternal instincts (and her suffering) for the audience: 'I had to bend down on the floor for breadcrumbs, I had to tear myself to pieces for what was not mine, but alien. Someone must be the helper' (89–90). Grusha realizes gradually that her hardships and sacrifice for

Michael's safety endear him to her. Brecht underscores this gradual realization by contrasting Michael – the 'noble child' – with Grusha's initial ignoble reluctance for her mission; at one point on her journey, Grusha even considers leaving the child behind.

Perhaps out of necessity she calls Michael her son for the first time in Scene 3, but by the time they are found and he is taken from her, Grusha actually believes it. As Scene 6 opens for the trial, she remarks with motherly affection upon seeing Michael again: 'He's so good. He can wash himself already' (114). This signals to us that she is thinking of his well-being before her own precarious situation and feels a sense of pride for raising him. And finally, we hear Grusha's definition of motherhood, which also doubles as her defence in front of the court (119–20). During the trial, Grusha conspicuously avoids hollow words like 'love' in her defence, invoked so insincerely by Natella's lawyers. Instead, she explains how actions and honesty define a mother, not meaningless phrases or mere biology. All this contrasts starkly with Natella's behaviour: from the beginning she considers the child a nuisance, as a thing to be groomed, and negligently hands him off to others. Grusha's deeds should resonate with us as much as they do for Azdak: Grusha acts like a mother whereas Natella pays lip service.

Azdak's final judgment deviates from the source material of the Chinese and biblical texts in a crucial way. While Brecht arrives at the same moral conclusions as the others, the Chinese and biblical stories still hold fast to the notion that the 'real' mother is the one who gave birth to the child. Brecht, however, disconnects biology and maternity. Azdak's judgment declares that the birth mother is a mother in name only and teaches us instead to ask a better question: isn't it in the best interest of the child that motherhood be determined by actions? As an audience, we observe not only how Azdak redefines motherhood but also the Brechtian position of looking at something in a different way. Here, Brecht makes a compelling argument for 'the children to the maternal' (128).

Azdak's verdict in this fairy-tale happy ending (uncommon for Brecht) should give us pause and signal that the rest is up to us. What follows must be a critical reassessment of our fundamental social structures with an eye to the future: being the change we want to see, holding true to our values, and altering society's priorities for the better. The final lines in the play from the Singer implore us to continue striving for change and social justice, for we must work in order to effect that change. What will it take to build a better, more equitable world for everyone?

Staging and Production

A designer, an actor, or a director would need to work diligently to bring this text to life on stage, either to reproduce the Brechtian devices discussed above or to reframe them for a contemporary audience (or both). The following brief points offer thoughts on how the play might be realized in performance without insisting on any one particular or appropriate rendering.

Scenography and props: The circle motif is integral to this play, so building such a circle, or perhaps a revolving stage, would create that space visually. The story has the characters constantly moving, so it is important to capture that kinetic energy on stage. One could envision either a fixed background or moving the play around the audience as a theatre in the round. Props could also be minimalist, instead opting for alternative visuals that suggest and imply rather than specify. Brecht used make-up and feudal wardrobe to bring out the social and class elements.

Songs and music: The songs are the glue that holds the play together and help to separate us from the play's storylines. The songs, accompanied by live music and perhaps choreography, would add to this effect.

Lighting: For the production at the Theater am Schiffbauerdamm, Brecht maintained a constant, even white light throughout the performance: this avoids illusion or an overt suggestion of atmosphere. Such a lighting scheme prevents shadow or sentiment and allows the audience to examine the play carefully.

Humour: Many characters in the play deliver witty one-liners and innuendo. Humour and precise language in Brecht's writing should not be forgotten. Laughter brings out both the didactic and entertainment value of the performance, and is often the result of the audience's response to *Verfremdung* – essentially the 'ah ha!' moment when we process dialogue or actions. Strangeness, disgust and exaggeration can cause laughter, too.

Historicization: A distinctive feature of epic theatre, even the most contemporary productions should consider this when staging the play. Historicizing emphasizes difference throughout time (political) and shows that actions and behaviours are relative rather than absolute (social). Simply giving a character an iPad instead of a pen and paper or including twentieth-century pop music neither updates the story nor fully accounts for the feudal setting. A contemporary staging could modernize the wardrobe for the characters and still historicize it if, for example, Grusha wore the uniform of a working-class woman and the Governor's Wife wore a power suit to highlight status. Historicization can also bring about *Verfremdung*.

Acting: Brecht insisted that his actors show that they are showing,[4] or perform to the audience rather than keep things internally or psychologically hidden. All decisions and details should be made visible and the actors should point to those arrangements on stage, for example in Scene 3. First, Grusha leaves Michael at the peasant couple's door because she cannot provide enough for him. Next, the Peasant Woman discovers the child and makes a series of decisions revealed to the audience: at first she is sceptical of the child's origins but is curious about him; however, upon seeing his fine linens (the mark of his class), she noticeably changes her viewpoint: children are expensive, especially this one (34). The actor shows the social and economic consequences of not accepting the child. Why isn't her sympathy for the helpless child instinctive? Because poor people cannot afford simple acts of charity. Acting that delivers epic theatre has less to do with method and more to do with stylizing. It is about experimentation and must be interpretive. It is all about taking a position or stance.

4 See Brecht, 'Showing Must be Shown!' *Collected Poems of Bertolt Brecht*. Eds and trans. David Constantine and Tom Kuhn. New York: Liveright, 2018. 921.

The Caucasian Chalk Circle

Collaborator: **R. Berlau**

Translators: **James and Tania Stern**, *with* **W. H. Auden**

Characters

Delegates of the Galinsk goat-breeding kolchos: an old peasant, a peasant woman, a young peasant, a very young workman · Members of the Rosa Luxemburg fruit-growing kolchos: an old peasant, a peasant woman, the agronomist, the girl tractor driver; the wounded soldier and other peasants from the kolchos · The expert from the capital · The singer Arkadi Cheidze · His musicians · Georgi Abashvili, the Governor · His wife, Natella · Their son, Michael · Shalva, the adjutant · Arsen Kazbeki, the fat prince · The rider from the capital · Niko Mikadze and Mikha Loladze, doctors · Simon Chachava, a soldier · Grusha Vachnadze, a kitchen-maid · Three architects · Four chambermaids: Assia, Masha, Sulika and Fat Nina · A nurse · A man cook · A woman cook · A stableman · Servants in the governor's palace · The governor's and the fat prince's Ironshirts and soldiers · Beggars and petitioners · The old peasant with the milk · Two elegant ladies · The innkeeper · The servant · A corporal · 'Blockhead', a soldier · A peasant woman and her husband · Three merchants · Lavrenti Vachnadze, Grusha's brother · His wife, Aniko · Their stableman · The peasant woman, for a time Grusha's mother-in-law · Yussup, her son · Brother Anastasius, a monk · Wedding guests · Children · Azdak, the village clerk · Shauva, a policeman · A refugee, the Grand Duke · The doctor · The invalid · The limping man · The blackmailer · Ludovica, the innkeeper's daughter-in-law · A poor old peasant woman · Her brother-in-law Irakli, a bandit · Three farmers · Illo Shaboladze and Sandro Oboladze, lawyers · The very old married couple

Scene One: The Struggle For the Valley

Among the ruins of a badly shelled Caucasian village the members of two kolchos villages are sitting in a circle, smoking and drinking wine. They consist mainly of women and old men, but there are also a few soldiers among them. With them is an expert of the State Reconstruction Commission from the capital.

A Peasant Woman (*left, pointing*) In those hills over there we stopped three Nazi tanks. But the apple orchard had already been destroyed.

An Old Peasant (*right*) Our beautiful dairy farm. All in ruins.

A Girl Tractor Driver (*left*) I set fire to it, Comrade. (*Pause.*)

The Expert Now listen to the report: the delegates of the Galinsk goat-breeding kolchos arrived in Nukha. When the Hitler armies were approaching, the kolchos had been ordered by the authorities to move its goat-herds further to the east. The kolchos now considers resettling in this valley. Its delegates have investigated the village and the grounds and found a high degree of destruction. (*The delegates on the right nod.*) The neighbouring Rosa Luxemburg fruit-growing kolchos (*to the left*) moves that the former grazing land of the Galinsk kolchos, a valley with scanty growth of grass, should be used for the replanting of orchards and vineyards. As an expert of the Reconstruction Commission, I request the two kolchos villages to decide between themselves whether the Galinsk kolchos shall return here or not.

An Old Man (*right*) First of all, I want to protest against the restriction of time for discussion. We of the Galinsk kolchos have spent three days and three nights getting here. And now we are allowed a discussion of only half a day.

A Wounded Soldier (*left*) Comrade, we no longer have as many villages and no longer as many working hands and no longer as much time.

The Girl Tractor Driver (*left*) All pleasures have to be rationed. Tobacco is rationed, and wine and discussion, too.

The Old Man (*right, sighing*) Death to the Fascists! But I will come to the point and explain to you why we want to have our valley back. There are a great many reasons, but I want to begin with one of the simplest. Makinae Abakidze, unpack the goat cheese.

A peasant woman, right, takes from a basket an enormous cheese wrapped in a cloth. Applause and laughter.

Help yourselves, comrades. Start in.

An Old Peasant (*left, suspiciously*) Is this meant to influence us, perhaps?

The Old Man (*right, amidst laughter*) How could it be meant as an influence, Surab, you valley-thief? Everyone knows that you will take the cheese and the valley, too. (*Laughter.*) All I expect from you is an honest answer: Do you like the cheese?

The Old Man (*left*) The answer is yes.

The Old Man (*right*) Oh. *Bitterly*. I might have guessed you know nothing about cheese.

The Old Man (*left*) Why not? When I tell you I like it!

The Old Man (*right*) Because you can't like it. Because it's not what it was in the old days. And why isn't it? Because our goats don't like the new grass as they used to like the old. Cheese is not cheese because grass is not grass, that's it. Mind you put that in your report.

The Old Man (*left*) But your cheese is excellent.

The Old Man (*right*) It's not excellent. Barely decent. The new grazing land is no good, whatever the young people may say. I tell you, it's impossible to live there. It doesn't even smell of morning there in the morning.

Several people laugh.

The Expert Don't mind their laughter. They understand you all the same. Comrades, why does one love one's country? Because the bread tastes better there, the sky is higher, the air smells better, voices sound stronger, the ground is easier to walk on. Isn't that so?

The Old Man (*right*) The valley has belonged to us for centuries.

The Soldier (*left*) What does that mean – for centuries? Nothing belongs to anyone for centuries. When you were young you didn't even belong to yourself, but to Prince Kazbeki.

The Old Man (*right*) According to the law the valley belongs to us.

The Girl Tractor Driver The laws will have to be re-examined in any case, to see whether they are still valid.

The Old Man (*right*) That's obvious. You mean to say it makes no difference what kind of tree stands beside the house where one was born? Or what kind of neighbour one has? Doesn't that make any difference? We want to go back just to have you next door to our kolchos, you valley-thieves. Now you can laugh that one off.

The Old Man (*left, laughing*) Then why don't you listen to what your 'neighbour', Kato Vachtang, our agronomist, has to say about the valley?

A Peasant Woman (*right*) We haven't said anywhere near all we have to say about our valley. Not all the houses are destroyed. At least the foundation wall of the dairy farm is still standing.

The Expert You can claim State support – both here and there. You know that.

A Peasant Woman (*right*) Comrade Expert, we're not trading now. I can't take your cap and hand you another, and say: 'This one's better.' The other one might be better, but you prefer yours.

The Girl Tractor Driver A piece of land is not like a cap. Not in our country, comrade.

The Expert Don't get angry. It's true that we have to consider a piece of land as a tool with which one produces something useful. But it's also true that we must recognize the love for a particular piece of land. Before we continue the discussion I suggest that you explain to the comrades of the Galinsk kolchos just what you intend to do with the disputed valley.

The Old Man (*right*) Agreed.

The Old Man (*left*) Yes, let Kato speak.

The Expert Comrade Agronomist!

The Agronomist (*rising. She is in military uniform*) Last winter, comrades, while we were fighting here in these hills as partisans, we discussed how after the expulsion of the Germans we could increase our orchards to ten times their former size. I have prepared a plan for an irrigation project. With the help of a dam on our mountain lake, three hundred hectares of unfertile land can be irrigated. Our kolchos could then grow not only more fruit, but wine as well. The project, however, would pay only if the disputed valley of the Galinsk kolchos could also be included. Here are the calculations. (*She hands* **The Expert** *a briefcase.*)

The Old Man (*right*) Write into the report that our kolchos plans to start a new stud farm.

The Girl Tractor Driver Comrades, the project was conceived during the days and nights when we had to take cover in the mountains and often were without ammunition for our few rifles. Even to get a pencil was difficult.

Applause from both sides.

The Old Man (*right*) Our thanks to the comrades of the Rosa Luxemburg kolchos and to all those who defended our country.

They shake hands and embrace.

The Peasant Woman (*left*) Our thoughts were that our soldiers – both your men and our men – should return to a still more fertile homeland.

The Girl Tractor Driver As the poet Mayakovsky said: 'The home of the Soviet people shall also be the home of Reason!'

The delegates on the right (*except* **The Old Man**) *have risen and, with the expert, study the agronomist's plans. Exclamations such as: 'Why is there a fall of 66 feet?' – 'This rock here is to be* *dynamited!' – 'Actually, all they need is cement and dynamite!' – 'They force the water to come down here, that's clever!'*

A Very Young Workman (*right, to* **The Old Man**, *right*) They are going to irrigate all the fields between the hills – look at that, Alleko.

The Old Man (*right*) I am not going to look at it. I knew the project would be good. I won't have a revolver pointed at my chest.

The Soldier But they are only pointing a pencil at your chest.

Laughter.

The Old Man (*right. He gets up gloomily and walks over to look at the drawings*) These valley-thieves know only too well that we can't resist machines and projects in this country.

The Peasant Woman (*right*) Alleko Bereshvili, you yourself are the worst one at new projects. That is well known.

The Expert What about my report? May I write that in your kolchos you will support the transfer of your old valley for the project?

The Peasant Woman (*right*) I will support it. What about you, Alleko?

The Old Man (*right, bent over the drawings*) I move that you give us copies of the drawings to take along.

The Peasant Woman (*right*) Then we can sit down to eat. Once he has the drawings and is ready to discuss them, the affair is settled. I know him. And it will be the same with the rest of us.

The delegates embrace again amidst laughter.

The Old Man (*left*) Long live the Galinsk kolchos and good luck to your new stud farm!

The Peasant Woman (*left*) Comrades, in honour of the visit of the delegates from the Galinsk kolchos and of the expert we have arranged a play featuring the singer Arkadi Cheidze, which has some bearing on our problem.

Applause.

The Girl Tractor *driver has gone off to fetch* **The Singer**.

The Peasant Woman (*right*) Comrades, your play will have to be good. We're going to pay for it with a valley.

The Peasant Woman (*left*) Arkadi Cheidze knows 21,000 verses by heart.

The Old Man (*left*) We rehearsed the play under his direction. It is very difficult to get him, by the way. You and the Planning Commission should see to it that he comes north more often, comrade.

The Expert We are more concerned with economy.

The Old Man (*left, smiling*) You arrange the new distribution of grapevines and tractors. Why not of songs, too?

Enter **The Singer** *Arkadi Cheidze, led by* **The Girl Tractor Driver**. *He is a sturdy man of simple manners, accompanied by musicians with their instruments. The artistes are greeted with applause.*

The Girl Tractor Driver This is the comrade expert, Arkadi.

The Singer *greets those round him.*

The Peasant Woman (*right*) I am very honoured to make your acquaintance. I've heard about your songs ever since I was at school.

The Singer This time it's a play with songs, and almost the whole kolchos takes part. We have brought along the old masks.

The Old Man (*right*) Is it going to be one of the old legends?

The Singer A very old one. It is called 'The Chalk Circle' and is derived from the Chinese. But we will recite it in a changed version. Yura, show the masks. Comrades, we consider it an honour to entertain you after such a difficult debate. We hope you will find that the voice of the old poet also sounds well in the shadow of Soviet tractors. It may be mistaken to mix different wines, but old and new wisdom mix very well. Now I hope we will all be given something to eat before the recital begins. That usually helps.

Voices Of course. – Everyone into the club house.

All go cheerfully to the meal. While they begin to move off, **The Expert** *turns to* **The Singer**.

The Expert How long will the story take, Arkadi? I have to get back to Tiflis tonight.

The Singer (*casually*) It is actually two stories. A few hours.

The Expert (*very confidentially*) Couldn't you make it shorter?

The Singer No.

Scene Two: The Noble Child

The Singer, *who is seen sitting on the floor in front of his musicians, a black sheepskin cloak round his shoulders, leafing through a small, well-thumbed script:*

Once upon a time
A time of bloodshed
When this city was called
The city of the damned
It had a Governor.
His name was Georgi Abashvili
Once upon a time.

He was very rich
He had a beautiful wife
He had a healthy child
Once upon a time.

No other governor in Grusinia
Had as many horses in his stable
As many beggars on his doorstep
As many soldiers in his service

As many petitioners in his courtyard
Once upon a time.

Georgi Abashvili, how shall I describe him?
He enjoyed his life:
On Easter Sunday morning
The Governor and his family went to church
Once upon a time.

Beggars and petitioners stream from a palace gateway, holding up thin children, crutches, and petitions. They are followed by two Ironshirts and then by **The Governor***'s family, elaborately dressed.*

The Beggars and Petitioners Mercy, Your Grace, the taxes are beyond our means . . . I lost my leg in the Persian War, where can I get . . . My brother is innocent, Your Grace, a misunderstanding . . . My child is starving in my arms . . . We plead for our son's discharge from the army, our one remaining son . . . Please, Your Grace, the water inspector is corrupt.

A servant collects the petitions, another distributes coins from a purse. Soldiers push back the crowd, lashing at it with thick leather whips.

Soldier Get back! Make way at the church door!

Behind **The Governor***, his wife and his Adjutant,* **The Governor***'s child is driven through the gateway in an ornate pram. The crowd surges forward to see it.*

The Singer (*while the crowd is driven back with whips*)
For the first time on this Easter Sunday, the people see the heir.
Two doctors never leave the child, the noble child
Apple of the Governor's eye.

Cries from the crowd: 'The child!' . . . 'I can't see it, stop pushing!' . . . 'God bless the child, Your Grace!'

The Singer
Even the mighty Prince Kazbeki
Bows before it at the church door.

A fat prince steps forward and bows before the family.

The Fat Prince Happy Easter, Natella Abashvili!

A command is heard. A rider arrives at the gallop and holds out to **The Governor** *a roll of documents. At a nod from* **The Governor The Adjutant***, a handsome young man, approaches the rider and stops him. There follows a brief pause during which* **The Fat Prince** *eyes the rider suspiciously.*

The Fat Prince What a magnificent day! While it was raining in the night I thought to myself: gloomy holidays. But this morning: a gay sky. I love a bright sky, a simple heart, Natella Abashvili. And little Michael, a governor from head to foot, tititi! (*He tickles the child.*) Happy Easter, little Michael, tititi!

The Governor's Wife What do you think of this, Arsen? Georgi has finally decided to start building the new wing on the east side. All these miserable slum houses are to be torn down to make room for a garden.

The Fat Prince That's good news after so much bad. What's the latest about the war, Brother Georgi? (**The Governor** *shows his lack of interest.*) A strategic retreat, I hear? Well, minor reverses invariably occur. Sometimes things go well, sometimes not so well. Such are the fortunes of war. Doesn't mean much, eh?

The Governor's Wife He's coughing! Georgi, did you hear?

(*Sharply to the two doctors, dignified men, who stand close to the pram:*) He's coughing!

First Doctor (*to the second*) May I remind you, Niko Mikadze, that I was against the lukewarm bath? A minor oversight in warming the bath water, Your Grace.

Second Doctor (*equally polite*) I can't possibly agree with you, Mikha Loladze. The temperature of the bath water was the one prescribed by our great and beloved Mishiko Oboladze. More likely a slight draught in the night, Your Grace.

The Governor's Wife But do take better care of him. He looks feverish, Georgi.

First Doctor (*bending over the child*) No cause for alarm, Your Grace. The bath water will be warmer. It won't happen again.

Second Doctor (*with a poisonous glance at the first*) I won't forget it, dear Mikha Loladze. No cause for alarm, Your Grace.

The Fat Prince Well, well, well! I always say: one pain in my liver and the doctor gets fifty strokes on the soles of his feet. And that's only because we live in such a decadent age. In the old days it would have been: Off with his head!

The Governor's Wife Let's go into the church. Very likely it's the draught here.

The procession, consisting of the family and servants, turns into the church doorway. **The Fat Prince** *follows.* **The Adjutant** *leaves the procession and points at the rider.*

The Governor Not before divine service, Shalva.

Adjutant (*to the rider*) The Governor doesn't want to be bothered with reports before the service – especially if they are, as I suspect, of a depressing nature. Go and get yourself something to eat in the kitchen, my friend.

The Adjutant *joins the procession while the rider enters the palace gateway, cursing. A soldier appears from the palace and remains standing in the gateway.*

The Singer

The city lies still.
On the church square the pigeons preen themselves.
A soldier of the palace guard
Is jesting with the kitchen maid
As she comes up from the river with a bundle.

A girl tries to pass through the gateway, a bundle of large green leaves under her arm.

The Soldier What! The young lady is not in church? Shirking service?

Grusha I was already dressed to go. But they wanted one more goose for the Easter banquet. And they asked me to fetch it. I know something about geese.

The Soldier A goose? (*Feigning suspicion.*) I'd like to see that goose.

Grusha *doesn't understand.*

One has to be on one's guard with women. They say: 'I only went to fetch a goose', and then it turns out to be something quite different.

Grusha (*walks resolutely towards him and shows him the goose*) There it is. And if it isn't a fifteen-pound goose, and they haven't stuffed it with corn, I'll eat the feathers.

The Soldier A queen of a goose. It will be eaten by the Governor himself. So the young lady has been down to the river again?

Grusha Yes, at the poultry farm.

The Soldier I see! At the poultry farm, down by the river. Not higher up, near those – those willows?

Grusha I go to the willows only to wash linen.

The Soldier (*insinuatingly*) Exactly.

Grusha Exactly what?

The Soldier (*winking*) Exactly that.

Grusha Why shouldn't I wash my linen near the willows?

The Soldier (*with exaggerated laughter*) 'Why shouldn't I wash my linen near the willows!' That's a good one, that is!

Grusha I don't understand the soldier. What's so good about it?

The Soldier (*slyly*) If someone knew what someone's told, she'd grow hot, she'd grow cold.

Grusha I don't know what I could know about those willows.

The Soldier Not even if there were a bush opposite? From which everything could be seen? Everything that happens there when a certain person is washing linen?

Grusha What happens there? Won't the soldier say what he means and have done with it?

The Soldier Something happens. And perhaps something can be seen.

Grusha Could the soldier mean that – once in a while on a hot day – I put my toes in the water? For otherwise there's nothing.

The Soldier And more – the toes and more.

Grusha More what? At most the foot.

The Soldier The foot and a little more. (*He laughs heartily.*)

Grusha (*angrily*) Simon Chachava, you ought to be ashamed of yourself! To sit in a bush on a hot day and wait till someone comes along and puts her leg in the river! And most likely with another soldier! (*She runs off.*)

The Soldier (*shouting after her*) Not with another soldier!

As **The Singer** *resumes his story* **The Soldier** *runs after* **Grusha.**

The Singer

The city lies still, but why are there armed men?
The Governor's palace lies at peace
But why is it a fortress?

From the doorway at the left **The Fat Prince** *enters quickly. He stands still and looks around. Before the gateway at the right two Ironshirts are waiting. Noticing them, the prince walks slowly past them, signs to them, then exits quickly. One Ironshirt exits through the gateway, the other remains on guard. Muffled voices come from different sides in the rear: 'To your posts!' The palace is surrounded. Distant church bells. Enter through the doorway the procession and* **The Governor**'*s family returning from church.*

The Singer

Then the Governor returned to his palace
Then the fortress was a trap
Then the goose was plucked and roasted
Then the goose was no longer eaten

Then noon was no longer the hour to eat
Then noon was the hour to die.

The Governor's Wife (*in passing*) It's quite impossible to live in this slum. But Georgi, of course, builds only for his little Michael. Never for me. Michael is everything, everything for Michael!

The Governor Did you hear Brother Kazbeki bid me a 'Happy Easter'? That's all very well, but so far as I know it didn't rain in Nukha last night. It rained where Brother Kazbeki was. Where was Brother Kazbeki?

The Adjutant That will have to be investigated.

The Governor Yes, at once. Tomorrow.

The procession turns into the gateway. The rider, who has meanwhile returned from the palace, walks towards **The Governor.**

The Adjutant Don't you want to listen to the rider from the capital, Your Excellency? He arrived this morning with confidential papers.

The Governor (*in passing*) Not before the banquet, Shalva!

The Adjutant (*to the rider, while the procession disappears into the palace and only two Ironshirts remain at the gate as palace guards*) The Governor doesn't wish to be disturbed by military reports before the banquet. The afternoon His Excellency will devote to conferences with prominent architects who have also been invited to the banquet. Here they are already. (*Enter three men. As the rider goes off,* **The Adjutant** *greets the architects.*) Gentlemen, His Excellency is awaiting you at the banquet. His entire time will be devoted to you. To the great new plans! Come, let us go!

One of the Architects We are impressed that his Excellency thinks of building in spite of the disquieting rumours that the war in Persia has taken a turn for the worse.

The Adjutant All the more reason for building! That's nothing. Persia is far away. The garrison here would let itself be chopped to pieces for its Governor.

Uproar from the palace. Shrill screams of a woman. Orders are shouted. Dumbfounded, **The Adjutant** *moves towards the gateway. An Ironshirt steps out and holds him up at the point of a lance.*

What's going on here? Put down that lance, you dog! (*To the palace guard, furiously.*) Disarm him! Can't you see an attempt is being made on the Governor's life?

The palace guard Ironshirts refuse to obey. Staring coldly, indifferently, at **The Adjutant**, *they watch the proceedings without interest.* **The Adjutant** *fights his way into the palace.*

One of the Architects The Princes! Don't you realize that the Princes met last night in the capital? And that they are against the Grand Duke and his governors? Gentlemen, we'd better make ourselves scarce.

They rush off.

The Singer

Oh, blindness of the great! They walk like gods
Great over bent backs, sure
Of hired fists, trusting
In their power which has already lasted so long.
But long is not forever.
Oh, Wheel of Fortune! Hope of the people!

From the gateway, enter **The Governor** *with a grey face, manacled, between two soldiers armed to the teeth.*

Walk, Your Highness, walk even now with head up.
From your Palace the eyes of many foes follow you!
You no longer need an architect, a carpenter will do.
You will not move into a new palace, but into a little hole in the ground.
Just look about you once more, you blind man!

The arrested **Governor** *looks about him.*

Does all you once possessed still please you? Between the Easter Mass and the banquet
You are walking to that place from which no one returns.

The Governor *is led away. The palace guard follows. A horn sounds. Noise behind the gateway.*

When the houses of the great collapse
Many little people are slain.
Those who had no share in the fortunes of the mighty
Often have a share in their misfortunes. The plunging wain
Drags the sweating beasts with it into the abyss.

Servants come rushing through the gateway in panic.

The Servants (*in confusion*) The hampers! – Take them all into the third courtyard! Food for five days! – Her Ladyship has fainted! Someone must carry her down. She must get away. – And what about us? We'll be slaughtered like chickens, it's the old story. – Jesus and Mary, what's going to happen? There's already bloodshed in the town, they say. – Nonsense, the Governor has just been asked politely to appear at a Princes' meeting. Everything'll be all right. I have this on the best authority.

The two doctors rush into the courtyard.

First Doctor (*trying to restrain the other*) Niko Mikadze, it is your duty as a doctor to attend Natella Abashvili.

Second Doctor My duty? It's yours!

First Doctor Niko Mikadze, who is in charge of the child today? You or me?

Second Doctor Do you really think, Mikha Loladze, I'm going to stay another minute in this cursed house for that little brat?

They start fighting. All one hears is: 'You neglect your duty!' and 'Duty be damned!' Then the **Second Doctor** *knocks down the first.*

Second Doctor Oh, go to hell! (*Exit.*)

The Servants There's time enough before night. The soldiers won't be drunk till then. – Does anyone know if they've started a mutiny yet? – The Palace Guard has ridden away. – Doesn't anyone know what's happened?

Grusha Meliva the fisherman says a comet with a red tail has been seen in the sky over the capital. That means bad luck.

The Servants Yesterday they were saying in the capital that the Persian War is lost. – The Princes have started a great revolt. There's a rumour that the Grand Duke has already fled. All his Governors are to be hanged. – The likes of us will be left alone. I have a brother in the Iron-shirts.

Enter the soldier **Simon Chachava**, *searching the crowd for* **Grusha.**

The Adjutant (*appearing in the doorway*) Everyone into the third courtyard! All hands help with the packing!

He drives **The Servants** *out.* **Simon** *finally finds* **Grusha.**

Simon There you are at last, Grusha! What are you going to do?

Grusha Nothing. If the worst comes to the worst, I've a brother with a farm in the mountains. But what about you?

Simon Don't worry about me. (*Polite again.*) Grusha Vachnadze, your desire to know my plans fills me with satisfaction. I've been ordered to accompany Madam Natella Abashvili as her guard.

Grusha But hasn't the Palace Guard mutinied?

Simon (*serious*) That they have.

Grusha But isn't it dangerous to accompany the woman?

Simon In Tiflis they say: how can stabbing harm the knife?

Grusha You're not a knife. You're a man, Simon Chachava. What has this woman to do with you?

Simon The woman has nothing to do with me. But I have my orders, and so I go.

Grusha The soldier is a pig-headed man; he gets himself into danger for nothing – nothing at all. (*As she is called from the palace:*) Now I must go into the third courtyard. I'm in a hurry.

Simon As there's a hurry we oughtn't to quarrel. For a good quarrel one needs time. May I ask if the young lady still has parents?

Grusha No, only a brother.

Simon As time is short – the second question would be: Is the young lady as healthy as a fish in water?

Grusha Perhaps once in a while a pain in the right shoulder; but otherwise strong enough for any work. So far no one has complained.

Simon Everyone knows that. Even if it's Easter Sunday and there's the question who shall fetch the goose, then it's she. The third question is this: Is the young lady impatient? Does she want cherries in winter?

Grusha Impatient, no. But if a man goes to war without any reason, and no message comes, that's bad.

Simon A message will come. (**Grusha** *is again called from the palace.*) And finally the main question . . .

Grusha Simon Chachava, because I've got to go to the third courtyard and I'm in a hurry, the answer is 'Yes'.

Simon (*very embarrassed*) Hurry, they say, is the wind that blows down the scaffolding. But they also say: The rich don't know what hurry is. – I come from . . .

Grusha Kutsk.

Simon So the young lady has already made inquiries? Am healthy, have no dependents, earn ten piastres a month, as a paymaster twenty, and am asking honourably for your hand.

Grusha Simon Chachava, that suits me.

Simon (*taking from his neck a thin chain from which hangs a little cross*) This cross belonged to my mother, Grusha Vachnadze. The chain is silver. Please wear it.

Grusha I thank you, Simon. (*He fastens it round her neck.*)

Simon Now I must harness the horses. The young lady will understand that. It would be better for the young lady to go into the third courtyard. Otherwise there'll be trouble.

Grusha Yes, Simon.

They stand together undecided.

Simon I'll just take the woman to the troops who've remained loyal. When the war's over, I'll come back. In two weeks. Or three. I hope my intended won't get tired waiting for my return.

Grusha Simon Chachava, I shall wait for you.

Go calmly into battle, soldier
The bloody battle, the bitter battle
From which not everyone returns.
When you return I will be there.
I will be waiting for you under the green elm
I will be waiting for you under the bare elm
I will wait until the last soldier has returned
And even longer.
When you return from the battle
No boots will lie before the door
The pillow beside mine will be empty
My mouth will be unkissed.
When you return, when you return
You will be able to say: all is as it was.

Simon I thank you, Grusha Vachnadze, and farewell!

He bows low before her; she bows low before him. Then she runs off without looking round. Enter **The Adjutant** *from the gateway.*

The Adjutant (*harshly*) Harness the horses to the big carriage! Don't stand there doing nothing, idiot!

Simon Chachava *leaps to attention and goes off. Two servants crawl in from the gateway, loaded down with heavy trunks. Behind them, supported by her women, stumbles Natella Abashvili. She is followed by another woman carrying Michael.*

The Governor's Wife As usual, nobody's paying the slightest attention. I hardly know if I'm standing on my head or my feet. Where's Michael? Don't hold him so clumsily! Pile the trunks on to the carriage! Shalva, is there any word from the Governor?

The Adjutant (*shaking his head*) You must get away at once.

The Governor's Wife Is there any news from the town?

The Adjutant No. So far all is quiet. But there isn't a minute to lose. There's not enough room for the trunks on the carriage. Please pick out what you need.

Exit **The Adjutant** *quickly.*

The Governor's Wife Only essentials! Quick, open the trunks. I'll tell you what I've got to have.

The trunks are lowered and opened.

The Governor's Wife (*pointing at some brocade dresses*) That green one! And of course that one with the fur trimming. Where are the doctors? I'm getting this terrible migraine again. It always starts in the temples. This one with the little pearl buttons . . . (*Enter* **Grusha**.) You're taking your time, eh? Go and get the hot water bottles at once!

Grusha *runs off, and returns with hot water bottles.* **The Governor's Wife** *orders her about by signs.*

The Governor's Wife (*watching a young woman attendant*) Don't tear the sleeve!

The Young Woman I promise you, madam, no harm has come to the dress.

The Governor's Wife Because I caught you. I've been watching you for a long time. Nothing in your head but making eyes at the Adjutant. I'll kill you, you bitch! (*She beats her.*)

The Adjutant (*returning*) I must ask you to make haste, Natella Abashvili. They are fighting in the town. (*Exit* **The Adjutant**.)

The Governor's Wife (*letting go of* **The Young Woman**) My God, do you think they'll do something to me? Why should they? (*All are silent. She herself begins to rummage in the trunks.*) Where's my brocade jacket? Help me! What about Michael? Is he asleep?

The Nurse Yes, madam.

The Governor's Wife Then put him down a moment and go and fetch my little morocco slippers from the bed-chamber. I need them to go with the green dress. (**The Nurse** *puts down the child and goes off. To* **The Young Woman**:) Don't stand around, you! (**The Young Woman** *runs off.*) Stay here, or I'll have you flogged! Just look at the way these things have been packed! No love! No understanding! If one doesn't give every order oneself. . . At such moments one realizes what one's servants are like! Masha! (*She gives her an order with a wave of the hand.*) You all gorge yourselves, but never a sign of gratitude! I won't forget this.

The Adjutant (*very excited*) Natella, you must leave at once! Orbeliani, Judge of the Supreme Court, has just been hanged! The carpet weavers are in revolt!

The Governor's Wife Why? I must have the silver dress – it cost 1,000 piastres. And that one there, and all my furs. And where's the wine-coloured dress?

The Adjutant (*trying to pull her away*) Riots have broken out in the outer town! We've got to leave this minute! (*A servant runs off.*) Where's the child?

The Governor's Wife (*to* **The Nurse**) Maro, get the child ready! Where are you?

The Adjutant (*leaving*) We'll probably have to do without the carriage. And ride.

The Governor's Wife *still rummages among her dresses, throws some on to the heap to go with her, then takes them off again. Drums are heard. The sky begins to redden.*

The Governor's Wife (*rummaging desperately*) I can't find that wine-coloured dress. (*Shrugging her shoulders, to* **The Second**

Woman:) Take the whole heap and carry it to the carriage. Why hasn't Maro come back? Have you all gone off your heads? I told you it's right at the bottom.

The Adjutant (*returning*) Quick! Quick!

The Governor's Wife (*to* **The Second Woman**) Run! Just throw them into the carriage!

The Adjutant We're not going by carriage. Come at once or I'll ride off on my own!

The Governor's Wife Maro! Bring the child! (*To* **The Second Woman**.) Go and look, Masha. No, first take the dresses to the carriage. It's all nonsense, I wouldn't dream of riding! (*Turning round, she sees the fire-reddened sky and starts back in horror.*) Fire! (*She rushes off, followed by* **The Adjutant**. **The Second Woman**, *shaking her head, follows with a heap of dresses. Servants enter from the gateway.*)

The Cook That must be the East Gate that's burning.

The Chef They've gone. And without the food wagon. How are we going to get away now?

A Stableman This is going to be an unhealthy place for some time. (*To the third chambermaid:*) Suleika, I'm going to fetch some blankets, we're clearing out.

The Nurse (*entering through the gateway with her mistress's slippers*) Madam!

A Fat Woman She's gone.

The Nurse And the child. (*She rushes to the child, and picks it up.*) They left it behind, those brutes! (*She hands the child to* **Grusha**.) Hold it for a moment. (*Deceitfully.*) I'm going to look for the carriage.

She runs off, following **The Governor's Wife.**

Grusha What have they done to the Governor?

The Stableman (*drawing his index finger across his throat*) Fft.

The Fat Woman (*seeing the gesture, becomes hysterical*) Oh God! Oh God! Oh God! Our master Georgi Abashvili! At morning Mass he was a picture of health! And now! Oh, take me away! We're all lost! We must die in sin! Like our master, Georgi Abashvili!

The Third Woman (*trying to calm her*) Calm down, Nina. You'll get away. You've done no one any harm.

The Fat Woman (*being led out*) Oh God! Oh God! Oh God! Let's all get out before they come! Before they come!

The Third Woman Nina takes it to heart more than the mistress. People like that get others even to do their weeping for them! (*Seeing the child in* **Grusha***'s arms.*) The child! What are you doing with it?

Grusha It's been left behind.

The Third Woman She just left it? Michael, who was never allowed to be in a draught!

The Servants *gather round the child.*

Grusha He's waking up.

The Stableman Better put him down, I tell you. I'd rather not think what'd happen to the person seen with that child. I'll get our things. You wait here. (*Exit into the palace.*)

The Cook He's right. Once they start they slaughter whole families. I'll go and fetch my belongings.

All go except **The Cook, The Third Woman** *and* **Grusha** *with the child in her arms.*

The Third Woman Didn't you hear? Better put him down!

Grusha The nurse asked me to hold him for a moment.

The Cook That one won't come back, you silly!

The Third Woman Keep your hands off him.

The Cook They'll be more after him than after his mother. He's the heir. Grusha, you're a good soul. But you know you're not too bright. I tell you, if he had the plague it couldn't be worse. Better see to it that you get away.

The Stableman *has come back carrying bundles which he distributes among the women. All except* **Grusha** *prepare to leave.*

Grusha (*stubbornly*) He hasn't got the plague. He looks at you like a human being.

The Cook Then don't you look back. You're just the kind of fool who always gets put upon. If someone says to you: Run and get the lettuce, you have the longest legs! – you run. We're taking the ox-cart, you can have a lift if you hurry. Jesus, by now the whole neighbourhood must be in flames!

The Third Woman Haven't you packed anything yet? There isn't much time, you know. The Ironshirts will soon be here from the barracks.

Exit both women and **The Stableman**.

Grusha I'm coming.

Grusha *lays the child down, looks at it for a moment, then takes clothes from the trunks lying about and covers the sleeping child. Then she runs into the palace to get her things. Sounds of horses' hoofs and of women screaming. Enter* **The Fat Prince** *with drunken Ironshirts. One of them carries the head of* **The Governor** *on a lance.*

The Fat Prince Put it here. Right in the middle! (*One Ironshirt climbs on to the back of another, takes the head and holds it over the gateway.*) That's not the middle. Further to the right. Good. What I do, my friends, I do well. (*While an Ironshirt with hammer and nail fastens the head by its hair:*) This morning at the church door I said to Georgi Abashvili: 'I love a clear sky'. Actually, what I prefer is lightning from a clear sky. Oh, yes. But it's a pity they took the brat away. I need him. Badly. Search the whole of Grusinia for him! 1,000 piastres reward!

As **Grusha** *enters cautiously through the doorway,* **The Fat Prince** *and the Ironshirts leave. Trampling of horses' hoofs again.*

Carrying a bundle, **Grusha** *walks towards the gateway. At the last moment, she turns to see if the child is still there. Promptly the singer begins to sing. She stands rooted to the spot.*

The Singer

As she was standing between courtyard and gate, she heard
Or thought she heard, a low voice. The child
Called to her, not whining but calling quite sensibly
At least so it seemed to her: 'Woman', it said, 'Help me'.
Went on calling not whining but calling quite sensibly:
'Don't you know, woman, that she who does not listen to a cry for help
But passes by shutting her ears, will never hear
The gentle call of a lover
Nor the blackbird at dawn, nor the happy
Sigh of the exhausted grape-picker at the sound of the Angelus.'
Hearing this

Grusha *walks a few steps towards the child and bends over it.*

she went back to the child
Just for one more look, just to sit with it
For a moment or two till someone should come
Its mother, perhaps, or someone else –

She sits down opposite the child, and leans against a trunk.

Just for a moment before she left, for now the danger was too great
The city full of flame and grief.

The light grows dimmer as though evening and night were falling, **Grusha** *has gone into the palace and fetched a lamp and some milk, which she gives the child to drink.*

The Singer (*loudly*)

Terrible is the temptation to do good!

Grusha *now settles down to keep watch over the child through the night. Once, she lights a small lamp to look at it. Once, she tucks it in with a brocade coat. Now and again she listens and looks up to see if someone is coming.*

For a long time she sat with the child.
Evening came, night came, dawn came.
Too long she sat, too long she watched
The soft breathing, the little fists
Till towards morning the temptation grew too strong.
She rose, she leaned over, she sighed, she lifted the child
She carried it off.

She does what **The Singer** *says as he describes it.*

Like booty she took it for herself
Like a thief she sneaked away.

Scene Three: The Flight Into the Northern Mountains

The Singer
As Grusha Vachnadze left the city
On the Grusinian highway
Towards the northern mountains
She sang a song, she bought some milk.

The Musicians
How will the merciful escape the merciless
The bloodhounds, the trappers?
Into the deserted mountains she wandered
Along the Grusinian highway she wandered
She sang a song, she bought some milk.

Grusha Vachnadze *continues on her way. On her back she carries the child in a sack, in one hand a bundle, in the other a big stick.*

Grusha (*singing*)
Four generals set off for Iran
Four generals but not one man.
The first did not strike a blow
The second did not beat the foe
For the third the weather was not right
For the fourth the soldiers would not fight.

Four generals went forth to attack
Four generals turned back.

Sosso Robakidse marched to Iran
Sosso Robakidse was a man.
He struck a sturdy blow
He certainly beat the foe
For him the weather was good enough
For him the soldiers fought with love
Sosso Robakidse marched to Iran
Sosso Robakidse is our man.

A peasant's cottage appears.

Grusha (*to the child*) Noontime, eating time. Now we'll sit here quietly in the grass, while the good Grusha goes and buys a little jug of milk. (*She lays the child down and knocks at the cottage door. An old peasant opens it.*) Grandpa, could I have a little mug of milk? And perhaps a corn cake?

The Old Man Milk? We haven't any milk. The soldiers from the city took our goats. If you want milk, go to the soldiers.

Grusha But Grandpa, you surely have a jug of milk for a child?

The Old Man And for a 'God Bless You', eh?

Grusha Who said anything about a 'God Bless You'? (*She pulls out her purse.*) We're going to pay like princes. Head in the clouds, bottom in the water! (*The peasant goes off grumbling to fetch milk.*) And how much is this jug?

The Old Man Three piastres. Milk has gone up.

Grusha Three piastres for that drop? (*Without a word* **The Old Man** *slams the door in her face.*) Michael, did you hear that? Three piastres! We can't afford that. (*She goes back, sits down again and gives the child her breast.*) Well, we must try again like this. Suck. Think of the three piastres. There's nothing there, but you think you're drinking, and that's something. (*Shaking her head, she realizes the child has stopped sucking. She gets up, walks* *back to the door, and knocks again.*) Open, Grandpa, we'll pay. (*Under her breath:*) May God strike you! (*When the old man appears again:*) I thought it would be half a piastre. But the child must have something. What about one piastre?

The Old Man Two.

Grusha Don't slam the door again. (*She rummages a long time in her purse.*) Here are two piastres. But this milk has got to last. We still have a long journey ahead of us. These are cutthroat prices. It's a sin.

The Old Man If you want milk, kill the soldiers.

Grusha (*letting the child drink*) That's an expensive joke. Drink, Michael. This is half a week's pay. The people here think we've earned our money sitting on our bottom. Michael, Michael, I certainly took on a nice burden with you! (*Looking at the brocade coat in which the child is wrapped:*) A brocade coat worth 1,000 piastres, and not one piastre for milk. (*She glances round.*) Look! There's a carriage, with rich ladies. We ought to get on to that.

In front of a caravansary. **Grusha** *dressed in the brocade coat is seen approaching two elegant ladies. She holds the child in her arms.*

Grusha Oh, you ladies want to spend the night here, too? It's awful how crowded it is everywhere! And not a carriage to be found! My coachman simply turned back. I've been walking half a mile on foot. Barefoot, too! My Persian shoes – you know those heels! But why doesn't someone come?

The Elder Lady That innkeeper certainly takes his time. The whole country has lost its manners since those goings-on started in the capital.

The Innkeeper *appears, a very dignified old man with a long beard, followed by his servant.*

The Innkeeper Excuse an old man for keeping you waiting, ladies. My little grandchild was showing me a peach tree in blossom. There on the slope, beyond the cornfields. We're planting fruit trees there, a few cherries. Further west (*pointing*) the ground gets more stony. That's where the farmers graze their sheep. You ought to see the peach blossom, the pink is exquisite.

The Elder Lady You live in a fertile region.

The Innkeeper God has blessed it. How far on is the fruit-blossom further south, my ladies? I take it you come from the south?

The Younger Lady I must admit I haven't been paying much attention to the landscape.

The Innkeeper (*politely*) Of course, the dust. It is advisable to travel slowly on our high roads. Provided, of course, one isn't in too great a hurry.

The Elder Lady Put your scarf round your throat, dearest. The evening breeze seems rather cool here.

The Innkeeper It comes down from the Janga-Tau glaciers, my ladies.

Grusha Yes, I'm afraid my son may catch cold.

The Elder Lady A very spacious caravansary! Shall we go in?

The Innkeeper Oh, the ladies want rooms? But the caravansary is full up, my ladies. And the servants have run off. I very much regret it, but I cannot accommodate another person, not even with references . . .

The Younger Lady But we can't spend the night here on the road.

The Elder Lady (*drily*) How much?

The Innkeeper My ladies, you will understand that in these times, when so many fugitives, no doubt quite respectable people but not popular with the authorities, are looking for shelter, a house has to be particularly careful. Therefore . . .

The Elder Lady My dear man, we aren't fugitives. We're simply moving to our summer residence in the mountains, that's all. It would never occur to us to ask for hospitality if – we needed it all that urgently.

The Innkeeper (*nodding his head in agreement*) Of course not. I only doubt if the tiny room at my disposal would suit the ladies. I have to charge 60 piastres per person. Are the ladies together?

Grusha In a way. I'm also in need of shelter.

The Younger Lady 60 piastres! That's a cut-throat price.

The Innkeeper (*coldly*) My ladies, I have no desire to cut throats. That's why . . . (*He turns to go.*)

The Elder Lady Must we talk about throats? Let's go in.

She enters, followed by **The Servant**.

The Younger Lady (*desperate*) 180 piastres for one room! (*Glancing back at* **Grusha**.) But with the child it's impossible! What if it cries?

The Innkeeper The room costs 180, whether it's two persons or three.

The Younger Lady (*changing her attitude to* **Grusha**) On the other hand, I couldn't bear to think of you on the road, my dear. Do come in.

They enter the caravansary. From the rear on the opposite side of the stage **The Servant** *appears with some luggage. Behind him come* **The Elder Lady**, **The Younger Lady** *and* **Grusha** *with the child.*

The Younger Lady 180 piastres! I haven't been so upset since they brought dear Igor home.

The Elder Lady Must you talk about Igor?

The Younger Lady Actually, we are four persons. The child is one too, isn't it? (*To* **Grusha**.) Couldn't you pay half at least?

Grusha That's impossible. I had to leave in a hurry, you see. And the Adjutant forgot to slip me enough money.

The Elder Lady Perhaps you haven't even got the 60?

Grusha That much I'll pay.

The Younger Lady Where are the beds?

The Servant There aren't any beds. Here are some sacks and blankets. You'll have to arrange them yourselves. Be glad you're not being put in a hole in the earth. Like lots of others. (*Exit.*)

The Younger Lady Did you hear that? I'm going straight to the innkeeper. That man must be flogged.

The Elder Lady Like your husband?

The Younger Lady Don't be so cruel! (*She weeps.*)

The Elder Lady How are we going to arrange something to sleep on?

Grusha I'll see to that. (*She puts down the child.*) It's always easier when there are several hands. You still have the carriage. (*Sweeping the floor.*) I was taken completely by surprise. 'My dear Anastasia Katarinovska,' my husband was saying before luncheon, 'do go and lie down for a while. You know how easily you get your migraine.' (*She spreads out sacks and makes beds. The ladies, watching her work, exchange glances.*) 'Georgi', said I to the Governor, 'I can't lie down when there are sixty for luncheon. And one can't trust the servants. And Michael Georgivich won't eat without me.' (*To* **Michael**:) See, Michael? Everything'll be all right, what did I tell you! (*She suddenly realizes that the ladies are watching her strangely and whispering.*) Well, there we are! At least one doesn't have to lie on the bare floor. I've folded the blankets double.

The Elder Lady (*imperiously*) You seem to be rather clever at making beds, my dear. Let's have a look at your hands!

Grusha (*frightened*) What?

The Younger Lady You're being asked to show your hands.

Grusha *shows the ladies her hands.*

The Younger Lady (*triumphant*) Cracked! A servant!

The Elder Lady (*goes to the door and shouts*) Service!

The Younger Lady You're caught! You swindler! Just confess what mischief you're up to!

Grusha (*confused*) I'm not up to any mischief. I just thought you might take us a little way in your carriage. Please, I ask you, don't make a noise, I'll go on my own.

The Younger Lady (*while* **The Elder Lady** *continues shouting for service*) Yes, you'll go all right, but with the police. For the moment you'll stay. Don't you dare move, you!

Grusha But I was ready to pay the 60 piastres. Here. (*She shows her purse.*) Look for yourself. I have them. Here are four tens, and here's a five – no, that's another ten, and ten, makes 60. All I want is to get the child on to the carriage. That's the truth.

The Younger Lady Aha, so that's what you want. On to the carriage! Now it's come out.

Grusha Madam, I confess, I am from a humble family. Please don't call the police. The child is of noble birth, look at the linen. It's fleeing, like yourself.

The Younger Lady Of noble birth! We know that one. The father's a prince, eh?

Grusha (*to* **The Elder Lady**, *fiercely*) Stop shouting! Have you no heart at all?

The Younger Lady (*to* **The Elder Lady**) Look out! She'll attack you! She's dangerous! Help! Murder!

The Servant (*entering*) What's going on here?

The Elder Lady This person here has smuggled herself in by playing the lady. She's probably a thief.

The Younger Lady And a dangerous one, too. She wanted to murder us. It's a case for the police. Oh God, I can feel my migraine coming on!

The Servant There aren't any police at the moment. (*To* **Grusha**.) Pack up your things, sister, and make yourself scarce.

Grusha (*angrily picking up the child*) You monsters! And they're already nailing your heads to the wall!

The Servant (*pushing her out*) Shut your trap. Or you'll have the Old Man here. And there's no trifling with him.

The Elder Lady (*to* **The Younger Lady**) Just see if she hasn't stolen something already!

While the ladies, right, look feverishly to see whether something has been stolen, **The Servant** *and* **Grusha** *go out through the door, left.*

The Servant Look before you leap, I say. Another time have a good look at people before you get mixed up with them.

Grusha I thought they'd be more likely to treat their own kind better.

The Servant Not them! Believe me, nothing's harder than aping a lazy useless person. Once they suspect you can wipe your own arse, or that your hands have ever touched a broom, the game's up. Just wait a minute, I'll get you a corn cake and a few apples.

Grusha Better not. I must get out before the Old Man comes. And if I walk all night I'll be out of danger, I think.

She walks away.

The Servant (*calling after her in a low voice*) At the next crossroads, turn right.

She disappears.

The Singer

As Grusha Vachnadze wandered northwards
She was followed by the Prince's Ironshirts.

The Musicians

How will the barefooted girl escape the Ironshirts
The bloodhounds, the trappers?
They are hunting even by night.
Pursuers don't get tired.
Butchers sleep little.

Two Ironshirts are trudging along the highway.

The Corporal Blockhead, you'll never amount to anything. Why? Because your heart's not in it. Your superior sees it in little things. Yesterday when I laid that fat woman, I admit you collared her husband as I commanded. And you did kick him in the stomach. But did you enjoy it like a good soldier? Or did you just do it from a sense of duty? I've kept my eyes on you, blockhead. You're like a hollow reed or a tinkling cymbal. You'll never get promoted. (*They walk awhile in silence.*) Don't you get the idea I don't notice how insubordinate you are in every way. I forbid you to limp! You do it simply because I sold the horses, and I sold them because I'd never have got that price again. I know you: you limp just to show me you don't like marching. But that won't help you. It'll go against you. Sing!

The Two Ironshirts (*singing*)

O sadly one morning, one morning in May
I kissed my darling and rode far away.
Protect her, dear friends, until home from the wars
I come riding in triumph, alive on my horse.

The Corporal Louder!

The Two Ironshirts

When I lie in my grave and my sword turns to rust
My darling shall bring me a handful of dust.
For the feet that so gaily ran up to her door
And the arms that went round her shall please her no more.

They begin to walk again in silence.

The Corporal A good soldier has his heart and soul in it. He lets himself be hacked to pieces by his superiors, and even while dying he's aware of his Corporal nodding approval. For him that's reward enough. That's all he wants. But *you* won't get a nod. And you'll croak just the same. Christ, how am I to lay my hands on the Governor's bastard with an ass like you!

They trudge on.

The Singer

When Grusha Vachnadze came to the River Sirra
The flight grew too much for her, the helpless child too heavy.

The Musicians

The rosy dawn in the cornfields
Is nothing but cold to the sleepless.
The gay clatter of the milk cans in the farmyard
Where the smoke rises is nothing but a threat to the fugitives.
She who drags the child feels nothing but its weight.

Grusha *stops in front of a farm.*

Grusha Now you've wetted yourself again, and you know I've no nappies. Michael, we've got to part. This is far enough from the city. They won't want you so badly, little squit, that they'll follow you all this way. The woman looks kind, and just you smell the milk! So farewell, little Michael. I'll forget how you kicked me in the back all night to make me go faster. And you – you forget the meagre fare. It was meant well. I'd love to have kept you, because your nose is so small, but it can't be done. I'd have shown you your first rabbit and – how not to wet yourself, but I must turn back, because my sweetheart the soldier might soon return, and suppose he didn't find me? You can't ask that of me, Michael.

A fat peasant woman carries a milk can to the door. **Grusha** *waits until she has gone in, then gingerly approaches the house. She tiptoes to the door and lays the child on the threshold. Then, hiding behind a tree, she waits until* **The Peasant Woman** *opens the door and sees the bundle.*

The Peasant Woman Jesus Christ, what's this? Husband!

The Peasant What's up? Let me have my soup.

The Peasant Woman (*to the child*) Where's your mother? Haven't you got one? It's a boy. And the linen is fine; it's from a good family. And they just leave him on our doorstep. Oh, what times we live in!

The Peasant If they think we're going to feed it, they're mistaken. You take it to the priest in the village. That's all we can do.

The Peasant Woman What will the priest do with it? It needs a mother. There, it's waking up. Don't you think we could keep it?

The Peasant (*shouting*) No!

The Peasant Woman I could lay it in the corner, next to the armchair. I only need a crib for it. And I can take it into the fields with me. Look how it's smiling! Husband, we have a roof over our heads and we can do it. I won't hear another word.

She carries the child into the house. **The Peasant** *follows, protesting.*

Grusha *steps out from behind the tree, laughs, and hurries away in the opposite direction.*

The Singer
Why so gay, you, making for home?

The Musicians
Because with a smile the child
Has won new parents for himself, that's why I'm gay.
Because I am rid of the loved one
That's why I'm happy.

The Singer
And why are you sad?

The Musicians
I'm sad because I'm single and free
Of the little burden in whom a heart was beating:
Like one robbed, like one impoverished I'm going.

Grusha *walks for a short while, then meets the two Ironshirts, who hold her up at the point of a lance.*

The Corporal Young lady, you're running into the Armed Forces. Where are you coming from? When are you coming? Are you entertaining illegal relations with the enemy? Where is he hiding? What sort of movements is he making in your rear? What about the hills? What about the valley? How are your stockings fastened?

Grusha *stands there frightened.*

Grusha They are strongly fastened; you'd better withdraw.

The Corporal I always withdraw. In that respect I'm reliable. Why are you staring like that at the lance? In the field a soldier never loses control of his lance. That's an order. Learn it by heart, blockhead. Now then, young lady, where are you off to?

Grusha To my intended, one Simon Chachava, of the Palace Guard in Nukha. Wait till I write to him; he'll break your bones for you.

The Corporal Simon Chachava? Indeed! I know him. He gave me the key so I could keep an eye on you once in a while. Blockhead, we're getting unpopular. We must make her realize we have honourable intentions. Young lady, my apparent flippancy hides a serious nature. So I'll tell you officially: I want a child from you.

Grusha *utters a little scream.*

Blockhead, she has understood. Ooh, isn't that a sweet fright! 'But first I must take the bread out of the oven, Officer! But first I must change my torn chemise, Colonel!' But joking apart. Listen, young lady, we are looking for a certain child in these parts. Have you heard of a child from the city, of good family, dressed in fine linen?

Grusha No. I've heard nothing.

The Singer

Run, kind heart! The killers are coming!
Help the helpless child, helpless girl! And so she runs.

Suddenly, panic-stricken, she turns round and runs. The Ironshirts glance at each other, then follow her, cursing.

The Musicians

In the bloodiest times
There are still good people.

As **Grusha** *enters the cottage,* **The Peasant Woman** *is bending over the child's crib.*

Grusha Hide it! Quick! The Ironshirts are coming! It was I who laid it on your doorstep. But it isn't mine. It's of a noble family.

The Peasant Woman Who's coming? What sort of Ironshirts?

Grusha Don't ask questions. The Ironshirts who are looking for it.

The Peasant Woman They've no business in my house. But it seems I must have a word with you.

Grusha Take off the fine linen. That will give us away.

The Peasant Woman Oh, you and your linen! In this house *I decide*. And don't you mess up my room. But why did you abandon it? That's a sin.

Grusha (*looking out of the window*) There, they're coming from behind the trees. I shouldn't have run away. That gave them ideas. What on earth shall I do?

The Peasant Woman (*looking out of the window and suddenly starting with fear*) Jesus and Mary! Ironshirts!

Grusha They're after the child!

The Peasant Woman But suppose they come in!

Grusha You mustn't give it to them. Say it's yours.

The Peasant Woman Yes.

Grusha They'll run it through if you let them have it.

The Peasant Woman But suppose they demand it? The money for the harvest is in the house.

Grusha If you let them have it, they'll run it through, here in your room! You've got to say it's yours.

The Peasant Woman Yes, but suppose they don't believe me?

Grusha You must speak firmly.

The Peasant Woman They'll burn the roof over our head.

Grusha That's why you've got to say it's yours. His name's Michael. I shouldn't have told you that.

The Peasant Woman *nods.*

Don't nod your head like that. And don't tremble; they'll notice.

The Peasant Woman Yes.

Grusha Stop saying yes. I can't stand it any longer. (*She shakes her.*) Haven't *you* got a child?

The Peasant Woman (*muttering*) In the war.

Grusha Then perhaps he's an Ironshirt, too, by now? And what if he ran children through? You'd give him a fine piece of your mind! 'Stop waving that lance in my room! Is that what I've reared you for? Go and wash your neck before you speak to your mother.'

The Peasant Woman That's true, I wouldn't let him behave like that.

Grusha Promise me you'll say it's yours.

The Peasant Woman Yes

Grusha There! They're coming!

There is a knocking at the door. The women don't answer. Enter the Ironshirts. **The Peasant Woman** *bows deeply.*

The Corporal Well, there she is. What did I tell you? My nose. I smelled her. Young lady, I have a question to ask you: Why did you run away? What did you think I would do to you? I'll bet it was something lewd. Confess!

Grusha (*while* **The Peasant Woman** *continues to bow*) I'd left the milk on the stove. Then I suddenly remembered it.

The Corporal I thought it was because you imagined I'd looked at you in a lewd way – as if I were thinking there could be something between us. A lustful glance, know what I mean?

Grusha I didn't see that.

The Corporal But it could have been, eh? You must admit that. After all, I could be a swine. I'm quite frank with you: I could think of all sorts of things if we were alone. (*To* **The Peasant Woman**.) Haven't you got something to do in the yard? The chickens to feed?

The Peasant Woman (*falling suddenly to her knees*) Soldier, I didn't known anything about it. Please don't set my house on fire.

The Corporal What are you talking about?

The Peasant Woman I have nothing to do with it. She left it on the doorstep, I swear.

The Corporal (*suddenly sees the child and whistles*) Ah, there's a little one in the crib! Blockhead, I smell a thousand piastres. Take the old girl out and hold on to her. It looks as though I'll have to do some cross-examining.

The Peasant Woman *lets herself be led out by the soldier, without a word.*

Well, there's the child I wanted to have from you. (*He walks towards the crib.*)

Grusha Officer, it's mine. It's not the one you're after.

The Corporal I'll just have a look at it. (*He bends over the crib.* **Grusha** *looks round in despair.*)

Grusha It's mine! It's mine!

The Corporal Nice linen!

Grusha *jumps at him to pull him away. He throws her off and again bends over the crib. Looking round in despair, she suddenly sees a big log of wood, seizes it in panic, and hits* **The Corporal** *over the head from behind. She quickly picks up the child and dashes off.*

The Singer

After her escape from the Ironshirts
After twenty-two days of wandering
At the foot of the Janga-Tau glacier
From this moment Grusha Vachnadze decided to be the child's mother.

The Musicians

The helpless girl
Became the mother of the helpless child.

Grusha *squats over a half-frozen stream to ladle some water in her hand for the child.*

Grusha

Nobody wants to take you
So I shall have to take you
There is no-one else but me, my dear
On this black day in a meagre year
Who will not forsake you.

Since I've carried you too long
And with sore feet
Since the milk was too dear
I grew fond of you.
(I wouldn't be without you any more.)

I'll throw your fine little shirt away
And wrap you in rags
I'll wash you and christen you
With glacier water.
(You'll have to bear it.)

She has taken off the child's fine linen and wrapped it in a rag.

The Singer

When Grusha Vachnadze, pursued by the Ironshirts
Came to the narrow footbridge of the Eastern slope
She sang the song of the rotten bridge
And risked two lives.

A wind has risen. The bridge on the glacier is visible in the semi-darkness. One rope is broken, and half the bridge is hanging down the precipice. Merchants, two men and a woman, stand undecided before the bridge as **Grusha** *and the child arrive. One man is trying to retrieve a hanging rope with a stick.*

The First Man Take your time, young woman. You won't get over that pass anyway.

Grusha But I simply have to get my child over to the east side. To my brother.

The Merchant Woman Have to? What d'you mean by have to ? I have to get there, too – because I have to buy two carpets in Atum

– carpets a woman had to sell because her husband had to die. But can I do what I have to; can she? Andrei has been fishing for two hours for that rope. And I ask you, how are we to fasten it, even if he gets it?

The First Man (*listening*) Shush, I think I hear something.

Grusha The bridge is not quite rotten. I think I'll try and cross it.

The Merchant Woman I wouldn't try that even if the devil himself were after me. It's suicide.

The First Man (*shouting*) Hi!

Grusha Don't shout! (*To* **The Merchant Woman**.) Tell him not to shout.

The First Man But someone down there's calling. Perhaps they've lost their way.

The Merchant Woman And why shouldn't he shout? Is there something wrong with you? Are they after you?

Grusha Well, I'll have to tell you. Ironshirts are after me. I knocked one down.

The Second Man Hide our merchandise!

The woman hides a sack behind a rock.

The First Man Why didn't you tell us that at once? (*To the other:*) If they catch her they'll make mincemeat out of her!

Grusha Get out of my way. I've got to cross that bridge.

The Second Man You can't. There's a precipice of two thousand feet.

The First Man Even if we could get the rope it wouldn't make sense. We could hold it with our hands, but then the Ironshirts could get across in the same way.

Grusha Out of my way.

Shouts from a distance: 'Let's get up there!'

The Merchant Woman They're getting near. But you can't take the child across that bridge. It's sure to break. Just look down!

Grusha *looks down the precipice. The Ironshirts are heard shouting below.*

The Second Man Two thousand feet!

Grusha But those men are worse.

The First Man Anyway you can't do it with the child. Risk your own life if they are after you, but not the child's.

The Second Man She's even heavier with the child.

The Merchant Woman Perhaps she's really got to go. Give it to me. I'll hide it and you cross the bridge alone.

Grusha I won't. We belong together. (*To the child:*) Live together, die together. (*She sings:*)

If the gulf is deep
And the rotten bridge sways
It is not for us, son
To choose our ways.

The way that I know
Is the one for your feet
The bread that I find
Is all you will eat.

Of every four morsels
You shall have three.
I would that I knew
How big they will be!

I'll try it.

The Merchant Woman That's tempting God.

Shouts from beneath.

Grusha I beg you, throw that stick away, or they'll get the rope and follow me.

She starts off on to the swinging bridge. **The Merchant Woman** *screams when the bridge looks like breaking. But* **Grusha** *walks on and reaches the far side.*

The First Man She's done it!

The Merchant Woman (*who has fallen on her knees and begun to pray, angrily*) But I still think it was a sin.

The Ironshirts appear, **The Corporal***'s head bandaged.*

The Corporal Have you seen a woman with a child?

The First Man (*while the second throws away his stick*) Yes, there she is! But the bridge won't carry you!

The Corporal Blockhead, you'll suffer for this!

Grusha, *from the far bank, laughs and shows the child to the Ironshirts. She walks on. The bridge is left behind. Wind.*

Grusha (*to the child*) You mustn't mind the wind. It's only a poor wretch, too. It has to push the clouds, and it feels the cold more than any of us. (*Snow starts falling.*) And the snow isn't the worst, Michael. It covers the little fir trees, so that they won't die in winter. And now I'll sing you a little song. Listen! (*She sings:*)

Your father's a thief
Your mother's a whore:
All the nice people
Will love you therefore.

The son of the tiger
Brings the foals their feed
The snake-child milk
To mothers in need.

Scene Four: In the Northern Mountains

The Singer
Seven days the sister wandered.
Across the glacier, down the hills she wandered.

'When I enter my brother's house', she thought to herself
'He will rise and embrace me'.
'Is that you, sister?' he will say
'I have been expecting you for so long. This here is my dear
wife.
And this is my farm, come to me by marriage.
With eleven horses and thirty-one cows. Sit down.
Sit down with your child at our table and eat.'
The brother's house was in a lovely valley.
When the sister came to the brother she was ill from her
wanderings.
The brother rose from the table.

A fat peasant couple who have just sat down to a meal. **Lavrenti Vachnadze** *already has a napkin round his neck, as* **Grusha**, *pale and supported by a stableman, enters with the child.*

Lavrenti Where do you come from, Grusha?

Grusha (*feebly*) I've walked across the Janga-Tau Pass, Lavrenti.

Stableman I found her in front of the hay barn. She has a child with her.

The Sister-in-Law Go and groom the roan. (*Exit* **Stableman**.)

Lavrenti This is my wife, Aniko.

The Sister-in-Law We thought you were in service in Nukha.

Grusha (*barely able to stand*) Yes, I was there.

The Sister-in-Law Wasn't it a good job? We were told it was a good one.

Grusha The Governor has been killed.

Lavrenti Yes, we heard there were riots. Your aunt told us about it. Remember, Aniko?

The Sister-in-Law Here, with us, it's quiet. City people always need some kind of excitement. (*She walks towards the door and shouts:*) Sosso, Sosso, take the flat cake out of the oven, d'you hear? Where are you? (*Exit, shouting.*)

Lavrenti (*quietly, quickly*) Has it got a father? (*As she shakes her head:*) I thought so. We must think up something. She's very pious.

The Sister-in-Law (*returning*) These servants! (*To* **Grusha:**) You have a child?

Grusha It's mine. (*She collapses.* **Lavrenti** *helps her up.*)

The Sister-in-Law Mary and Joseph, she's ill – what are we to do?

Lavrenti *tries to lead* **Grusha** *to the bench by the stove. Aniko waves her away in horror and points to the sack by the wall.*

Lavrenti (*escorting her to the wall*) Sit down, sit down. I think it's just weakness.

The Sister-in-Law As long as it's not scarlet fever.

Lavrenti Then she'd have spots. I'm sure it's only weakness. Don't worry, Aniko. (*To* **Grusha**:) Do you feel better sitting ?

The Sister-in-Law Is the child hers?

Grusha It's mine.

Lavrenti She's on her way to her husband.

The Sister-in-Law Really? Your meat's getting cold. (**Lavrenti** *sits down and begins to eat.*) Cold food's not good for you. At least the fat parts mustn't get cold; you know your stomach's your weak spot. (*To* **Grusha**:) If your husband's not in town, where is he then?

Lavrenti She got married on the other side of the mountain, she says.

The Sister-in-Law Oh, on the other side. (*She also sits down to eat.*)

Grusha I think I'll have to lie down somewhere, Lavrenti.

The Sister-in-Law (*goes on questioning her*) If it's consumption we'll all get it. Has your husband a farm?

Grusha He's a soldier.

Lavrenti But he's coming into a farm – a small farm from his father.

The Sister-in-Law Isn't he in the war? Why not?

Grusha (*wearily*) Yes, he's in the war.

The Sister-in-Law Then why d'you want to go to the farm?

Lavrenti When he comes back from the war, he'll come to his farm.

The Sister-in-Law But you're going there now?

Lavrenti Yes, to wait for him.

The Sister-in-Law (*shrilly*) Sosso, the cake!

Grusha (*murmurs in fever*) A farm – a soldier – waiting – sit down – eat.

The Sister-in-Law That's scarlet fever.

Grusha (*starting up*) Yes, he has a farm!

Lavrenti I think it must be weakness, Aniko. Wouldn't you like to go and look after the cake yourself, my dear?

The Sister-in-Law But when will he come back if the war, as they say, has broken out again? (*Waddling away, shouting:*) Sosso! Where are you? Sosso!

Lavrenti (*getting up quickly and going to* **Grusha**) You'll get a bed in a moment. She has a good heart. But only after supper.

Grusha (*holding out the child to him*) Take it. *He takes it, looking anxiously round.*

Lavrenti But you can't stay here long. You must realize she's very pious.

Grusha *collapses.* **Lavrenti** *takes hold of her.*

The Singer

The sister was too ill.
The cowardly brother had to give her shelter.
The autumn passed, the winter came.
The winter was long
The winter was short.

The people mustn't know.
The rats mustn't bite
The spring mustn't come.

Grusha *sits bent at the weaving loom in the scullery. She and the child, who squats on the floor, are wrapped in blankets.*

Grusha (*sings while weaving*)
Then the lover started to leave
Then his girl ran pleading after him
Pleading and crying, crying and pleading:
Dearest mine, dearest mine
As you now go into battle
As you now have to fight the enemy
Don't throw yourself into the front line
And don't push with the rear line.
In front is red fire
In the rear is red smoke.
Stay wisely in between
Keep near the standard bearer.
The first ones always die
The last ones are also hit
Those in the centre come home.

Michael, we must be clever. If we make ourselves really small, like cockroaches, our sister-in-law will forget we're in the house. Then we can stay here till the snow melts. And don't cry because of the cold. Being poor and cold as well puts people off.

Enter **Lavrenti**. *He sits down beside* **Grusha**.

Lavrenti Why are you two sitting there muffled up like coachmen? Perhaps it's too cold in the room?

Grusha (*hastily removing her shawl*) It's not too cold, Lavrenti.

Lavrenti If it's too cold, you oughtn't to sit here with the child. Aniko would blame herself. (*Pause.*) I hope the priest didn't question you about the child.

Grusha He did, but I didn't tell him anything.

Lavrenti That's good. I wanted to talk to you about Aniko. She has a good heart – but she's very, very sensitive. People only have to mention our farm and she's worried. She takes everything to heart, you know. Our milkmaid once went to church with a hole in her stocking. Ever since then my dear Aniko has always worn two pairs of stockings to church. It's hard to believe, but it's the old family in her. (*He listens.*) Are you sure there are no rats here? If so, you couldn't stay here. (*Sounds of drops from the roof.*) What's that dripping?

Grusha Must be a barrel leaking.

Lavrenti Yes, it must be a barrel. Now you've already been here six months, haven't you? Was I talking about Aniko? Of course I didn't mention the Ironshirt. She has a weak heart. That's why she doesn't know you can't look for work. And that's why she made those remarks yesterday. (*They listen again to the melting snow.*) Can you believe it? She's worrying about your soldier. 'Suppose he comes back and doesn't find her!' she says, and lies awake. 'He can't come before the spring,' I tell her. The dear woman! (*The drops begin to fall faster.*) When d'you think he'll come? What's your idea? (**Grusha** *is silent.*) Not before the spring. That's what you think, too? (**Grusha** *is silent.*) I see you no longer believe he'll come back. (**Grusha** *does not answer.*) But when spring comes and the snow is melting on the passes you must leave here. Because then they can come and look for you. People are already talking about a child with an unmarried mother.

The beat of the falling drops has grown faster and steadier.

Grusha, the snow is melting on the roof and spring is here.

Grusha Yes.

Lavrenti (*eagerly*) Let me tell you what we'll do. You need a place to go to. And because of the child (*he sighs*) you must have a husband, to stop people talking. I've made cautious inquiries about how we can get a husband for you, Grusha, and I've found one. I talked to a woman who has a son, just over the mountain, a little farm. She's willing.

Grusha But I can't marry another man! I must wait for Simon Chachava.

Lavrenti Of course. That's all been considered. You don't need a man in bed, but a man on paper. And that's the very man I've found. The son of the woman I spoke to is dying. Isn't that wonderful? He's just at his last gasp. And everything's as we have said: A man just over the mountain! And when you reached him he died, and so you're a widow. What do you say?

Grusha I could do with a stamped up document for Michael.

Lavrenti A stamp makes all the difference. Without a stamp even the Shah of Persia couldn't prove he is the Shah. And you'll have a roof over your head.

Grusha How much does she want for it?

Lavrenti 400 piastres.

Grusha Where will you find the money?

Lavrenti (*guiltily*) Aniko's milk money.

Grusha No-one will know us over there. I'll do it.

Lavrenti (*gets up*) I'll tell the woman at once. (*Exit quickly.*)

Grusha Michael, you cause a lot of trouble. I came by you as the pear tree comes by the sparrows. And because a Christian bends down and picks up a crust of bread so it won't go to waste. Michael, I ought to have walked away quickly on that Easter Sunday in Nukha. Now I'm the fool.

The Singer

The bridegroom was lying on his deathbed, when the bride arrived.
The bridegroom's mother was waiting at the door, bidding them hurry.
The bride brought along a child, the witness hid it during the wedding.

A space divided by a partition. On one side a bed. Under the mosquito net lies a very sick man. On the other side **The Mother-in-Law** *rushes in pulling* **Grusha** *after her. They are followed by* **Lavrenti** *and the child.*

The Mother-in-Law Quick! Quick! Or he'll die on us before the wedding. (*To* **Lavrenti**:) But I was never told she already had a child.

Lavrenti What's it matter? (*Pointing towards the dying man:*) It's all the same to him in his condition.

The Mother-in-Law Him? But I won't survive the shame. We're honest people. (*She begins to weep.*) My Yussup doesn't have to marry someone who already has a child.

Lavrenti All right, I'll add another 200 piastres. You have it in writing that the farm will go to you; but she has the right to live here for two years.

The Mother-in-Law (*drying her tears*) It will hardly cover the funeral expenses. I hope she will really lend me a hand with the work. And now what's happened to the monk? He must have slipped out by the kitchen window. When they get wind in the village that Yussup's end is near, they'll all be round our necks. Oh dear! I'll go and get the monk. But he mustn't see the child.

Lavrenti I'll take care he doesn't see it. But why a monk? Why not a priest?

The Mother-in-Law Oh, he's just as good. I made one mistake: I paid him half his fee in advance. Now he'll have gone to the tavern. I hope . . . (*She runs off.*)

Lavrenti She saved on the priest, the wretch! She's hired a cheap monk.

Grusha Send Simon Chachava to me if he turns up.

Lavrenti Yes. (*Glancing at the sick man:*) Won't you have a look at him?

Grusha, *taking* **Michael** *to her, shakes her head.*

He's not moving an eyelid. I hope we aren't too late.

They listen. On the opposite side enter neighbours, who look round and take up positions against the walls. They start muttering prayers. Enter **The Mother-in-Law** *with* **The Monk**.

The Mother-in-Law (*surprised and angry, to* **The Monk**) Now we're for it! (*She bows to the guests.*) I must ask you to wait a few moments. My son's bride has just arrived from town and we've got to have an emergency wedding. (*She goes with* **The Monk** *into the bedchamber.*) I knew you'd spread it about. *To* **Grusha**: The wedding can start at once. Here's the licence. I and the bride's brother (**Lavrenti** *tries to hide in the background, after having quickly taken* **Michael** *away from* **Grusha. The Mother-in-Law** *beckons him away from the child*) the bride's brother and I are the witnesses.

Grusha *has bowed to* **The Monk**. *They approach the bed:* **The Mother-in-Law** *lifts the mosquito-net:* **The Monk** *begins babbling the marriage service in Latin. Meanwhile* **The Mother-in-Law** *beckons to* **Lavrenti** *to get rid of the child, but* **Lavrenti**, *fearing that the child will cry, draws its attention to the ceremony.* **Grusha** *glances once at the child, and* **Lavrenti** *makes the child wave to her.*

The Monk Are you prepared to be a faithful, obedient and good wife to this man? And to cleave to him until death you do part?

Grusha (*looking at the child*) Yes.

The Monk (*to the dying man*) And are you prepared to be a good and loving husband to your wife until death you do part?

As the dying man does not answer, **The Monk** *repeats the question, then looks round.*

The Mother-in-Law Of course he is! Didn't you hear him say yes?

The Monk All right. We declare this marriage contracted. Now what about Extreme Unction?

The Mother-in-Law Nothing doing! The wedding was quite expensive enough. I must now take care of the mourners. (*To* **Lavrenti**.) Did we say 700?

Lavrenti 600. (*He pays.*) Now I don't want to sit and get acquainted with the guests. So farewell, Grusha. And if my widowed sister comes to visit me one day, she'll get a 'welcome' from my wife. Or I'll get disagreeable.

He leaves. The mourners glance after him without interest.

The Monk And may one ask whose this child is?

The Mother-in-Law Is there a child? I don't see any child. And you don't see one either – understand? Or else I've seen all kinds of things happening behind the tavern! Come along now.

They move back to the room. After **Grusha** *has put down the child and told it to be quiet, she is introduced to the neighbours.*

This is my daughter-in-law. She arrived just in time to find dear Yussup still alive.

One of the Women He's been ill now a whole year, hasn't he? When my Vassili was called up he was there to say goodbye.

Another Woman Such things are terrible for a farm. With the corn ripe on the stalk and the farmer in bed! It will be a blessing for him if he doesn't suffer much longer, I say.

First Woman (*confidentially*) At first we thought he took to his bed because of military service, you know. And now his end is coming.

The Mother-in-Law Please sit down and have some cakes.

She beckons to **Grusha** *and both women go into the bedroom, where they pick up trays of cakes from the floor. The guests, among them* **The Monk**, *sit on the floor and begin conversing in subdued voices.*

A Very Old Peasant (*to whom* **The Monk** *has slipped the bottle he has taken from his cassock*) There's a little one, you say! How can Yussup have managed that?

Third Woman Anyway, she was lucky to have brought it off in time, with him so sick.

The Mother-in-Law They are gossiping already. And stuffing themselves with the funeral cakes at the same time. And if he doesn't die today, I'll have to bake fresh ones tomorrow.

Grusha I'll bake them.

The Mother-in-Law When some riders passed by last night, and I went out to see who they were, he was lying there like a corpse! That's why I sent for you. It can't take much longer. (*She listens.*)

The Monk Dear wedding guests and mourners! We stand deeply moved in front of a bed of death and marriage, because the bride gets into bed and the groom into the grave. The groom is already washed, and the bride is already hot. For in the marriage-bed lies the last Will, and that makes people randy. Oh, my children, how varied is the fate of man! The one dies to get a roof over his head, and the other marries so that flesh may be turned to dust, from which it was made. Amen.

The Mother-in-Law (*who had listened*) He's got his own back. I shouldn't have hired such a cheap one. That's what you'd expect. An expensive one knows how to behave. In Sura there's one who is even in the odour of sanctity; but of course he charges a fortune. A fifty-piastre priest like this one here has no dignity. And as for piety, he has precisely fifty piastres' worth, and no more. And when I fetched him from the tavern he was just finishing a speech and shouting: 'The war is over, beware of the peace!' We must go in.

Grusha (*giving* **Michael** *a cake*) Eat this cake and be a good boy, Michael. We are respectable now.

The two women carry the trays of cakes to the guests. The dying man is sitting up in bed; he puts his head out from under the mosquito-net and watches the two women. Then he sinks back again. **The Monk** *takes two bottles from his cassock and offers them to the peasant beside him. Enter three musicians, to whom* **The Monk** *waves with a grin.*

The Mother-in-Law (*to the musicians*) What have you got your instruments for?

A Musician Brother Anastasius here (*pointing at* **The Monk**) told us there was a wedding going on.

The Mother-in-Law What! You brought them? Three more on my neck! Don't you know there's a dying man next door?

The Monk That's a tempting task for an artist. They could play a hushed Wedding March or a gay Funeral Dance.

The Mother-in-Law Well, you might as well play. I can't stop you eating, in any case.

The musicians play a musical medley. The women offer cakes.

The Monk The trumpet sounds like a whining baby. And you, little drum, what gossip are you spreading abroad?

A Peasant (*beside* **The Monk**) What about the bride shaking a leg?

The Monk Shake the legs or rattle the bones?

The Peasant (*beside* **The Monk**, *singing*)
When pretty Miss Plushbottom wed
A rich man with no teeth in his head
They enquired, 'Is it fun?'
She replied, 'No, it's none.
Still, there're candles and soon he'll be dead.'

The Mother-in-Law *throws the drunken man out. The music stops. The guests are embarrassed. Pause.*

The Guests (*loudly*) Have you heard the latest? The Grand Duke's back! – But the Princes are against him. – Oh, the Shah of Persia, they say, has lent him a great army, to restore order in Grusinia. – How is this possible? After all, the Shah of Persia is against the Grand Duke! – But against disorder, too. – In any case, the war's over. Our soldiers are already coming back.

Grusha *drops the tray of cakes.*

An Old Woman (*to* **Grusha**) Are you feeling ill? That's just excitement about dear Yussup. Sit down and rest awhile, my dear.

Grusha *stands, swaying.*

The Guests Now everything will be as it was. Only the taxes will go up because we'll have to pay for the war.

Grusha (*weakly*) Did someone say the soldiers are back?

A Man I did.

Grusha That can't be true.

The Man (*to a woman*) Show her the shawl. We bought it from a soldier. It's from Persia.

Grusha (*looking at the shawl*) They are here.

A long pause. **Grusha** *kneels as if to pick up the cakes. As she does so she takes the silver cross and chain out of her blouse, kisses it, and starts praying.*

The Mother-in-Law (*while the guests silently watch* **Grusha**) What's the matter with you? Won't you look after our guests? What's all this nonsense from the city got to do with us?

The Guests (*resuming their conversation while* **Grusha** *remains with her forehead bent to the ground*) Persian saddles can be bought from soldiers, but some exchange them for crutches. – Only one side's bigwigs can win, but the soldiers on both sides are the losers. – At least the war's over now. It's something that they can't call you up any more. – (*The dying man sits bolt upright in bed. He listens.*) – What we need most are two weeks of good weather. – There's hardly a pear on our trees this year.

The Mother-in-Law (*offering the cakes*) Have some more cake. And enjoy it. There's more to come.

The Mother-in-Law *goes to the bedroom with empty trays. Unaware of the dying man, she bends down to pick up some more cakes, when he begins to talk in a hoarse voice.*

Yussup How many more cakes are you going to stuff down their throats? D'you think I can shit money? (**The Mother-in-Law** *starts, and stares at him aghast, while he puts his head out from behind the mosquito-net.*) Did they say the war was over?

First Woman (*talking kindly to* **Grusha** *in the next room*) Has the young woman someone in the war?

The Man That's good news that they're on their way home, eh?

Yussup Don't stare so! Where's the wife you've foisted on me?

Receiving no answer, he climbs out of bed and in his nightshirt staggers past his mother into the other room. Trembling, she follows him with the cake tray.

The Guests (*seeing him and shrieking*) Jesus, Mary and Joseph! Yussup!

Everyone leaps up in alarm. The women rush to the door. **Grusha**, *still on her knees, turns round and stares at* **The Man**.

Yussup The funeral supper! That's what you'd like! Get out before I kick you out!

The guests stampede from the house.

Yussup (*grumpily to* **Grusha**) That puts a spoke in your wheel, eh?

Receiving no answer, he turns round and takes a cake from the tray which his mother holds.

The Singer

Oh, confusion! The wife discovers that she has a husband!
By day there's the child, by night there's the man.
The lover is on his way day and night.
The married couple are looking at each other. The chamber is
narrow.

Yussup *sits naked in a high wooden bathtub. His mother pours water from a jug. Next door in the bedroom* **Grusha** *squats with* **Michael**, *who is playing at mending a straw mat.*

Yussup That's her business, not yours. Where's she hiding now?

The Mother-in-Law (*calling*) Grusha! The peasant wants you!

Grusha (*to* **Michael**) There are still two holes to mend.

Yussup (*as* **Grusha** *enters*) Scrub my back!

Grusha Can't the peasant do that himself?

Yussup 'Can't the peasant do that himself?' Get the brush! To hell with you! Are you the wife or are you a stranger? (*To* **The Mother-in-Law**:) Too cold!

The Mother-in-Law I'll run and get some more hot water.

Grusha Let me do it.

Yussup You stay here. (**The Mother-in-Law** *goes out.*) Rub harder. And don't make such a fuss. You've seen a naked man before. That child of yours can't have come out of thin air.

Grusha The child was not conceived in joy, if that's what the peasant means.

Yussup (*turning and grinning*) A likely story! (**Grusha** *stops scrubbing him and starts back. Enter* **The Mother-in-Law**.) This is a nice thing you've saddled me with here! A cold-fish for a wife!

The Mother-in-Law She isn't willing.

Yussup Pour – but go easy! Ow! Go easy, I said. (*To* **Grusha**.) I'd be surprised if you hadn't been up to something in the city. What else would you be here for? But I won't say anything about that. I also haven't said anything about the bastard you brought into my house. But my patience with you is coming to an end. It's against nature. (*To* **The Mother-in-Law**.) More! (*To* **Grusha**.) And even if your soldier does return, you're married.

Grusha Yes.

Yussup But your soldier won't return now. Don't you believe it.

Grusha No.

Yussup You're cheating me. You're my wife and you're not my wife. Where you lie, nothing lies. And yet no other woman can lie there. When I go to work in the mornings I'm dead-tired. When I lie down at night I'm awake as the devil. God has made you a woman, and what d'you do about it? My fields don't bring me in enough to buy myself a woman in town. Besides, it's a long way. Woman hoes the fields and parts her legs. That's what our almanac says. D'you hear?

Grusha Yes. (*Quietly.*) I don't like cheating you out of it.

Yussup She doesn't like! Pour some more water. (**The Mother-in-Law** *pours.*) Ow!

The Singer

As she sat by the stream to wash the linen
She saw his image in the water, and his face grew dimmer
As the months passed by.
As she raised herself to wring the linen
She heard his voice from the murmuring maple, and his voice grew fainter
As the months passed by.
Excuses and sighs grew more numerous, tears and sweat flowed faster
As the months passed by, as the child grew up.

Grusha *sits by a stream dipping linen into the water. Some distance away a few children are standing.* **Grusha** *is talking to* **Michael**.

Grusha You can play with them, Michael. But don't let them order you about because you're the smallest.

Michael *nods and joins the children. They start playing.*

The Tallest Boy Today we're going to play Heads-off. (*To a fat boy:*) You're the Prince and you must laugh. (*To* **Michael**:) You're the Governor. (*To a girl:*) You're the Governor's wife and you cry when his head's chopped off. And I do the chopping. (*He shows his wooden sword.*) With this. First, the Governor's led into the courtyard. The Prince walks ahead. The Governor's wife comes last.

They form a procession. **The Fat Boy** *goes ahead, and laughs. Then comes* **Michael**, *and* **The Tallest Boy**, *and then the girl, who weeps.*

Michael (*standing still*) Me too chop head off!

The Tallest Boy That's my job. You're the smallest. The Governor's part is easiest. All you do is kneel down and have your head chopped off. That's simple.

Michael Me too have sword.

The Tallest Boy That's mine. (*He gives him a kick.*)

The Girl (*shouting to* **Grusha**) He doesn't want to do what he's told.

Grusha (*laughing*) Even ducklings take to water, they say.

The Tallest Boy You can play the Prince if you know how to laugh.

Michael *shakes his head.*

The Fat Boy I'm the best laugher. Let him chop off the head just once. Then you do it, then me.

Reluctantly **The Tallest Boy** *hands* **Michael** *the wooden sword and kneels.* **The Fat Boy** *sits down, smacks his thigh and laughs with all his might. The girl weeps loudly.* **Michael** *swings the big sword and chops off the head. In doing so, he topples over.*

The Tallest Boy Hi, I'll show you how to do it properly.

Michael *runs away, and the children run after him.* **Grusha** *laughs, following them with her eyes. On turning round, she sees* **Simon Chachava** *standing on the opposite bank. He wears a shabby uniform.*

Grusha Simon!

Simon Is that Grusha Vachnadze?

Grusha Simon!

Simon (*politely*) A good morning, and good health to the young lady.

Grusha (*gets up gaily and bows deeply*) A good morning to the soldier. And thank God he has returned in good health.

Simon They found better fish than me, so they didn't eat me, said the haddock.

Grusha Courage, said the kitchen boy. Luck, said the hero.

Simon And how are things here? Was the winter bearable? Did the neighbour behave ?

Grusha The winter was a little rough, the neighbour as usual, Simon.

Simon May one ask if a certain person is still in the habit of putting her leg in the water when washing her linen?

Grusha The answer is no. Because of the eyes in the bushes.

Simon The young lady is talking about soldiers. Here stands a paymaster.

Grusha Is that worth twenty piastres?

Simon And board.

Grusha (*with tears in her eyes*) Behind the barracks under the date trees.

Simon Just there. I see someone has kept her eyes open.

Grusha Someone has.

Simon And has not forgotten. (**Grusha** *shakes her head.*) And so the door is still on its hinges, as they say. (**Grusha** *looks at him in silence and shakes her head again.*) What's that mean? Is something wrong?

Grusha Simon Chachava, I can never go back to Nukha. Something has happened.

Simon What has happened?

Grusha It so happened that I knocked down an Ironshirt.

Simon Grusha Vachnadze will have had her reasons for that.

Grusha Simon Chachava, my name is also no longer what it was.

Simon (*after a pause*) I don't understand that.

Grusha When do women change their names, Simon? Let me explain it to you: Nothing stands between us. Everything between us has remained as it was. You've got to believe that.

Simon How can nothing stand between us and things be changed?

Grusha How can I explain it to you? So fast and with the stream between us? Couldn't you cross that bridge?

Simon Perhaps it's no longer necessary.

Grusha It's most necessary. Come over, Simon. Quick!

Simon Is the young lady saying that someone has come too late?

Grusha *looks up at him in despair, her face streaming with tears.*

Simon *stares before him. He picks up a piece of wood and starts cutting it.*

The Singer

So many words are said, so many words are left unsaid.
The soldier has come. Whence he comes he doesn't say.
Hear what he thought but didn't say:
The battle began at dawn, grew bloody at noon.
The first fell before me, the second behind me, the third at my side.
I trod on the first, I abandoned the second, the captain sabred the third.
My one brother died by steel, my other brother died by smoke.
My neck was burnt by fire, my hands froze in my gloves, my toes in my socks.

For food I had aspen buds, for drink I had maple brew, for bed I had stones in water.

Simon I see a cap in the grass. Is there a little one already?

Grusha There is, Simon. How could I hide it? But please don't let it worry you. It's not mine.

Simon They say: Once the wind begins to blow, it blows through every crack. The woman need say no more.

Grusha *lowers her head and says no more.*

The Singer

There was great yearning but there was no waiting.
The oath is broken. Why was not disclosed.
Hear what she thought, but didn't say:
While you fought in the battle, soldier

The bloody battle, the bitter battle
I found a child who was helpless
And hadn't the heart to do away with it.
I had to care for what otherwise would have come to harm
I had to bend down on the floor for breadcrumbs
I had to tear myself to pieces for what was not mine
But alien.
Someone must be the helper.
Because the little tree needs its water
The little lamb loses its way when the herdsman is asleep
And the bleating remains unheard.

Simon Give me back the cross I gave you. Or better, throw it in the stream.

He turns to go.

Grusha Simon Chachava, don't go away. It isn't mine, it isn't mine! (*She hears the children calling.*) What is it, children?

Voices Soldiers have come! – They are taking Michael away!

Grusha *stands aghast as two Ironshirts, with* **Michael** *between them, come towards her.*

Ironshirt Are you Grusha? (*She nods.*) Is that your child?

Grusha Yes. (**Simon** *goes off.*) Simon!

Ironshirt We have official orders to take this child, found in your charge, back to the city. There is suspicion that it is Michael Abashvili, son and heir of the late Governor Georgi Abashvili, and his wife, Natella Abashvili. Here is the document and the seal.

They lead the child away.

Grusha (*running after them and shouting*) Leave it here, please! It's mine!

The Singer
The Ironshirts took the child away, the precious child.
The unhappy girl followed them to the city, the dangerous place.
The real mother demanded the child back. The foster mother

faced her trial.
Who will try the case, on whom will the child be bestowed?
Who will be the Judge? A good one, a bad one?
The city was in flames. On the Judgment Seat sat Azdak.

Scene Five: The Story of the Judge

The Singer
Listen now to the story of the Judge:
How he turned Judge, how he passed judgment, what kind of Judge he is.
On the Easter Sunday of the great revolt, when the Grand Duke was overthrown
And his Governor Abashvili, father of our child, lost his head
The village clerk Azdak found a fugitive in the woods and hid him in his hut.

Azdak, *in rags and tipsy, helps a fugitive dressed as a beggar into his hut.*

Azdak Don't snort. You're not a horse. And it won't do you any good with the police if you run like a dirty nose in April. Stop, I tell you. (*He catches* **The Fugitive**, *who has trotted into the hut as though he would go through the walls.*) Sit down and feed: here's a piece of cheese. (*From under some rags in a chest he fishes out some cheese, and* **The Fugitive** *greedily begins to eat.*) Haven't had anything for some time, eh? (**The Fugitive** *groans.*) Why did you run so fast, you arse-hole? The police wouldn't even have seen you!

The Fugitive Had to.

Azdak Blue funk? (**The Fugitive** *stares, uncomprehending.*) Got the squitters? Afraid? Don't slobber like a Grand Duke or a sow. I can't stand it. It's well-born stinkers we've got to put up with as God made them. Not the likes of you. I once heard of a Senior Judge who farted at a public dinner. Just to show his independence. Watching you eat like that really gives me the most awful ideas! Why don't you say something? (*Sharply.*) Let's have a look at your hand. Can't you hear? Show me your hand. (**The Fugitive** *slowly puts out his hand.*) White! So you're no beggar at all! A fraud! A swindle on legs! And here am I hiding you from the police as though you were a decent human being! Why run like that if you're a landowner? Because that's what you are. Don't try to deny it. I see it in your guilty face. (*He gets up.*) Get out of here! (**The Fugitive** *looks uncertainly at him.*) What are you waiting for, you peasant-flogger?

The Fugitive Am hunted. Ask for undivided attention. Make proposition.

Azdak What do you want to make? A proposition? Well, if that isn't the height of insolence! He making a proposition! The bitten man scratches his fingers bloody, and the leech makes a proposition. Get out, I tell you!

The Fugitive Understand point of view. Persuasion. Will pay 100,000 piastres for one night. How's that?

Azdak What? Do you think you can buy me? And for 100,000 piastres? A third-rate farm. Let's say 150,000. Got it?

The Fugitive Not on me, of course. Will be sent. Hope, don't doubt.

Azdak Doubt profoundly! Get out!

The Fugitive *gets up and trots to the door. A voice from off-stage.*

Voice Azdak!

The Fugitive *turns, trots to the opposite corner and stands still.*

Azdak (*shouting*) I'm not in. (*He walks to the door.*) Is that you spying around here again, Shauva?

Policeman Shauva (*outside, reproachfully*) You've snared another rabbit, Azdak. You promised me it wouldn't happen again.

Azdak (*severely*) Shauva, don't talk about things you don't understand. The rabbit is a dangerous and destructive animal. It devours plants, especially what they call weeds. So it must be exterminated.

Shauva Azdak, don't be so hard on me. I'll lose my job if I don't arrest you. I know you have a good heart.

Azdak I *don't* have a good heart! How often am I to tell you I'm a man of intellect?

Shauva (*slyly*) I know, Azdak. You're a superior person. You say so yourself. I'm a Christian and I've no education. So I ask you: if one of the Prince's rabbits is stolen, and I'm a policeman, what am I to do with the offender?

Azdak Shauva, Shauva, shame on you! There you stand asking me a question. Nothing is more tempting than a question. Suppose you were a woman – let's say Nunovna, that bad girl – and you showed me your thigh – Nunovna's thigh, that is – and you asked me: what shall I do with my thigh? It itches. Is she as innocent as she pretends? No. I catch a rabbit, you catch a man. Man is made in God's image. Not so a rabbit, you know that. I'm a rabbit-eater; but you're a man-eater, Shauva. And God will pass judgment on you. Shauva, go home and repent. No, stop! There's something . . . (*He looks at* **The Fugitive**, *who stands trembling in the corner.*) No, it's nothing after all. Go home and repent. (*He slams the door behind* **Shauva**. *To* **The Fugitive**:) Now you're surprised, eh? Surprised I didn't hand you over? But I couldn't hand over even a bedbug to that beast of a policeman! It goes against my grain. Don't tremble at the sight of a policeman. So old and yet so cowardly! Finish your cheese, but eat it like a poor man, or else they'll still catch you. Do I even have to tell you how a poor man behaves? (*He makes him sit down, and then gives him back the cheese.*) The box is the table. Put your elbows on the table, and now surround the plate with your arms as though you expected the cheese to be snatched from you at any moment. What right have you to be safe? Now hold the knife as if it were a small sickle; and don't look so greedily at your cheese, look at it mournfully – because it's already disappearing – like all good things. (**Azdak** *watches him.*) They're after you. That speaks in your favour. But how can I be sure they're not mistaken about you? In Tiflis they once hanged a landowner, a Turk. He could prove he quartered his peasants instead of merely cutting them in half, as is the custom.

And he squeezed twice the usual amount of taxes out of them. His zeal was above all suspicion, and yet they hanged him like a common criminal. Why? Because he was a Turk – something he couldn't do much about. An injustice! He got on to the gallows like Pontius Pilate into the Creed. In a word, I don't trust you.

The Singer

Thus Azdak gave shelter to the old beggar
Only to find out that he was that murderer, the Grand Duke.
And he was ashamed of himself, he accused himself and
 ordered the policeman
To take him to Nukha, to Court, to be judged.

In the Court of Justice three Ironshirts sit drinking. From a pillar hangs a man in judge's robes. Enter **Azdak**, *in chains, dragging* **Shauva** *behind him.*

Azdak (*shouting*) I have helped the Grand Duke, the Grand Thief, the Grand Murderer, to escape! In the name of Justice, I demand to be judged severely in a public trial!

The First Ironshirt Who is this queer bird?

Shauva That's our clerk, Azdak.

Azdak I am despicable, treacherous, branded! Tell them, flatfoot, how I insisted on being put in chains and brought to the capital. Because I sheltered the Grand Duke, the Grand Swindler, by mistake. As I realized only afterwards when I found this document in my hut. (*The Ironshirts study the document. To* **Shauva**:) They can't read. Point out that the branded man is accusing himself. Tell them how I forced you to walk with me through half the night, to get everything cleared up.

Shauva And all by threats. That wasn't nice of you, Azdak.

Azdak Shauva, shut your trap. You don't understand. A new age has come, which will thunder over you. You're finished. The police are being wiped out, pfft! Everything is being investigated, brought into the open. In which case a man prefers to give himself up. Why? Because he won't escape the mob. Tell them how I've been shouting all along Shoemaker Street! (*He acts with expansive* *gestures, looking sideways at the Ironshirts.*) 'Out of ignorance I let the Grand Swindler escape. Tear me to pieces, brothers!' So as to get in first.

The First Ironshirt And what was their answer?

Shauva They comforted him in Butcher Street, and laughed themselves sick in Shoemaker Street. That's all.

Azdak But here with you it's different, I know you're men of iron. Brothers, where is the Judge? I must be tried.

The First Ironshirt (*pointing at the hanged man*) Here's the Judge. And stop 'brothering' us. That's rather a sore spot this evening.

Azdak 'Here's the Judge.' That's an answer never heard in Grusinia before. Citizens, where's His Excellency the Governor? (*Pointing at the gallows:*) Here's His Excellency, stranger. Where's the Chief Tax Collector? Where's the official Recruiting Officer? The Patriarch? The Chief of Police? Here, here, here – all here. Brothers, that's what I expected from you.

The Second Ironshirt Stop! What did you expect, you bird?

Azdak What happened in Persia, brothers. What happened there.

The Second Ironshirt And what did happen in Persia?

Azdak Forty years ago. Everyone hanged. Viziers, tax-collectors. My grandfather, a remarkable man, saw it all. For three whole days. Everywhere.

The Second Ironshirt And who reigned after the Vizier was hanged?

Azdak A peasant.

The Second Ironshirt And who commanded the army?

Azdak A soldier, soldier.

The Second Ironshirt And who paid the wages?

Adazk A dyer. A dyer paid the wages.

The Second Ironshirt Wasn't it a carpet weaver perhaps?

The First Ironshirt And why did all this happen, you Persian?

Azdak 'Why did all this happen?' Must there be a special reason? Why do you scratch yourself, brother? War! Too long a war! And no justice! My grandfather brought back a song that tells what it was all about. I and my friend the policeman will sing it for you. (*To* **Shauva**:) And hold on to the rope, that's part of it. (*He sings, with* **Shauva** *holding the rope.*)

Why don't our sons bleed any longer, why don't our daughters weep any more?
Why do only the calves in the slaughterhouse have any blood, why only willows on Lake Urmi tears?
The Grand King must have a new province, the peasant must relinquish his savings.
In order to capture the roof of the world, the cottage roofs have to be torn down.
Our men are scattered in all directions, so that the great ones can eat at home.
The soldiers kill each other, the marshals salute each other.
The widow's tax money has to be fingered to see if it's good, the swords break.
The battle has been lost, but the helmets have been paid for.
Is that right? Is that right?

Shauva Yes, yes, yes, yes, yes, that's right.

Azdak Do you want to hear the whole thing?

The First Ironshirt *nods.*

The Second Ironshirt (*to* **Shauva**) Did he teach you that song?

Shauva Yes. Only my voice isn't good.

The Second Ironshirt No. (*To* **Azdak**:) Go on singing.

Azdak The second verse is about the peace. (*He sings*:)

The offices are jammed, the officials are working in the streets.
The rivers overflow their banks and lay waste the fields.
Those incapable of letting down their own trousers rule countries.

Those who can't count up to four devour eight courses.
The corn farmers look round for buyers, but see only the starving.
The weavers go home from their looms in rags.
Is that right? Is that right?

Shauva Yes, yes, yes, yes, yes, that's right.

Azdak

That's why our sons bleed no longer, our daughters weep no more.
That's why only the calves in the slaughterhouse have any blood.
And the willows in the morning on Lake Urmi have any tears.

The First Ironshirt (*after a pause*) Are you going to sing that song here in town?

Azdak Of course. What's wrong with it?

The First Ironshirt Do you see the sky getting red? (*Turning round,* **Azdak** *sees the sky reddened by fire.*) That's in the outer town. This morning when Prince Kazbeki had Governor Abashvili beheaded our carpet weavers also caught the 'Persian disease'. They asked if Prince Kazbeki isn't eating too many courses. And this afternoon they strung up the town judge. But we beat them to pulp for two piastres per weaver, you understand?

Azdak (*after a pause*) I understand.

He glances shyly round and, creeping away, sits down in a corner, his head in his hands.

The First Ironshirt (*to the third, after they have all had a drink*) Just wait and see what'll happen next.

The first and second Ironshirts walk towards **Azdak** *and block his exit.*

Shauva I don't think he's a really bad character, gentlemen. He poaches a few chickens here and there, and perhaps an odd rabbit.

The Second Ironshirt (*approaching* **Azdak**) You've come here to fish in troubled waters, eh?

Azdak (*looking up*) I don't know why I've come here.

The Second Ironshirt Do you happen to be in with the carpet weavers? (**Azdak** *shakes his head.*) And what about this song?

Azdak From my grandfather. A stupid, ignorant man.

The Second Ironshirt Right. And what about the dyer who paid the wages?

Azdak That was in Persia.

The First Ironshirt And what about denouncing yourself for not having hanged the Grand Duke with your own hands?

Azdak Didn't I tell you that I let him escape?

Shauva I swear to it. He let him escape.

The Ironshirts *drag* **Azdak** *screaming to the gallows. Then they let him loose and burst out laughing.* **Azdak** *joins in the laughter, laughing loudest. They then unchain him. They all start drinking. Enter* **The Fat Prince** *with a young man.*

The First Ironshirt (*to* **Azdak**) There you have your new age.

More laughter.

The Fat Prince And what is there to laugh about here, my friends? Permit me a serious word. Yesterday morning the Princes of Grusinia overthrew the Grand Duke's war-thirsty government and did away with his governors. Unfortunately the Grand Duke himself escaped. In this fateful hour our carpet weavers, these eternal troublemakers, had the audacity to incite a rebellion and hang our universally beloved city Judge, our dear Illa Orbeliani. Tuttut. My friends, we need peace, peace, peace in Grusinia. And justice. Here I bring you my dear nephew, Bizergan Kazbeki. He's to be the new Judge, a talented fellow. I say: the people must decide.

The First Ironshirt Does this mean we elect the Judge?

The Fat Prince Precisely. The people propose a talented fellow. Confer, my friends. (*The Ironshirts confer.*) Don't worry, little fox. The job's yours. And once we've run the Grand Duke to earth we won't have to kiss the rabble's arse any more.

The Ironshirts (*each other*) They've got the jitters because they still haven't caught the Grand Duke. – We've this clerk to thank for that. He let him get away. – They're not sure of things yet. So they say: 'My friends!' And: 'The people must decide!' – Now he even wants justice for Grusinia! – But fun's fun as long as it lasts. – We'll ask the clerk; he knows all about justice. Hey, scoundrel . . .

Azdak You mean me?

The First Ironshirt (*continues*) Would you like to have the nephew as Judge?

Azdak You asking me? You're not really asking me that, are you?

The Second Ironshirt Why not? Anything for a laugh!

Azdak I take it you want him put to the test? Am I right? Have you a crook on hand? An experienced one? So the candidate can show how good he is?

The Third Ironshirt Let me see. We have the Governor's tarts' two doctors down there. Let's use them.

Azdak Stop! That's no good! You can't take real crooks till we're sure of the Judge being appointed. He may be an ass, but he must be appointed or else the law is violated. The law is a very sensitive organ. Like the spleen. Once attacked with fists, death occurs. You can hang those two. Why not? You won't have violated the law, because no Judge was present. Judgment must always be passed with complete solemnity – because it's such rot. Suppose a Judge throws a woman into clink for having stolen a corncake for her child. And he isn't wearing his robes. Or he's scratching himself while passing sentence so that more than a third of his body is exposed – in which case he'd have to scratch his thigh – then the sentence he passes is a disgrace and the law is violated. It would be easier for a Judge's robe and a Judge's hat to pass sentence than for a man without all that paraphernalia. If you don't look out, the law goes up in smoke. You don't taste wine by offering it to a dog. Why not? Because the wine would be gone.

The First Ironshirt So what do you suggest, you hair-splitter?

Azdak I'll be the defendant. I even know what sort. (**Azdak** *whispers to them.*)

The First Ironshirt You? (*All burst out laughing.*)

The Fat Prince What have you decided?

The First Ironshirt We've decided to have a rehearsal. Our good friend will act as defendant, and here's the Judge's seat for the candidate.

The Fat Prince That's unusual. But why not? (*To* **The Nephew**.) A mere formality, little fox. What did they teach you? Who gets there first? The slow runner or the fast one?

The Nephew The silent one, Uncle Arsen.

The Nephew *sits in the Judge's seat,* **The Fat Prince** *standing behind him.* **The Ironshirts** *sit on the steps. Enter* **Azdak**, *imitating the unmistakeable gait of the Grand Duke.*

Azdak Is there anyone here who knows me? I am the Grand Duke.

The Fat Prince What is he?

The Second Ironshirt The Grand Duke. He really does know him.

The Fat Prince Good.

The First Ironshirt Get on with the proceedings.

Azdak Listen! I'm accused of war-mongering. Ridiculous! Am saying: ridiculous! Is that enough? If not, have brought lawyers along. About 500. (*He points behind him, pretending to be surrounded by lawyers.*) Requisition all available seats for lawyers. (*The Ironshirts laugh;* **The Fat Prince** *joins in.*)

The Nephew (*to the Ironshirts*) Do you want me to try this case? I must admit I find it rather unusual. From the point of view of taste, I mean.

The First Ironshirt Go on.

The Fat Prince (*smiling*) Let him have it, little fox!

The Nephew All right. People of Grusinia versus Grand Duke. What have you to say, defendant?

Azdak Any amount. Of course, have myself read war lost. Started war at the time on advice of patriots like Uncle Kazbeki. Demand Uncle Kazbeki as witness. (*The Ironshirts laugh.*)

The Fat Prince (*to the Ironshirts, affably*) Quite a card, eh?

The Nephew Motion overruled. You're being accused not of declaring war, which every ruler has to do once in a while, but of conducting it badly.

Azdak Rot! Didn't conduct it at all! Had it conducted. Had it conducted by Princes. Made a mess of it, of course.

The Nephew Do you deny having been Commander in Chief?

Azdak Not at all. Always was Commander in Chief. Even at birth ticked off wet-nurse; dismissed turds promptly in potty. Got used to command. Always commanded officials to rob my cash-box. Officers flog soldiers only on my command. Landlords sleep with peasant's wives only when strictly commanded by me. Uncle Kazbeki here grew stomach only on my command.

The Ironshirts (*clapping*) He's good! Up the Grand Duke!

The Fat Prince Answer him, little fox! I'm with you!

The Nephew I shall answer him according to the dignity of the law. Defendant, preserve the dignity of the law.

Azdak Agreed. Command you proceed with the trial.

The Nephew It's not your business to command me. So you claim the Princes forced you to declare war. Then how can you claim they made a mess of it?

Azdak Didn't send enough troops. Embezzled funds. Brought sick horses. During attack found drunk in whorehouse. Propose Uncle Kaz as witness. (*The Ironshirts laugh.*)

The Nephew Are you making the outrageous claim that the Princes of this country did not fight?

Azdak No. Princes fought. Fought for war contracts.

The Fat Prince (*jumping up*) That's too much! This man talks like a carpet weaver!

Azdak Really? Only telling the truth!

The Fat Prince Hang him! Hang him!

The First Ironshirt Keep quiet. Get on, Excellency.

The Nephew Quiet! Now pass sentence. Must be hanged. Hanged by the neck. Having lost war. Sentence passed. No appeal.

The Fat Prince (*hysterically*) Away with him! Away with him! Away with him!

Azdak Young man, seriously advise not to fall publicly into jerky, clipped manner of speech. Can't be employed as watchdog if howl like wolf. Got it?

The Fat Prince Hang him!

Azdak If people realize Princes talk same language as Grand Dukes, may even hang Grand Dukes and Princes. By the way, sentence quashed. Reason: war lost, but not for Princes. Princes have won *their* war. Got themselves paid 3,863,000 piastres for horses not delivered.

The Fat Prince Hang him!

Azdak 8,240,000 piastres for food supplies not produced.

The Fat Prince Hang him!

Azdak Are therefore victors. War lost only for Grusinia, which is not present in this Court.

The Fat Prince I think that's enough, my friends. (*To* **Azdak**:) You can withdraw, gaol-bird. (*To the Ironshirts*:) I think you can now ratify the new Judge's appointment, my friends.

The First Ironshirt Yes, we can do that. Take down the Judge's robe. (*One of the Ironshirts climbs on the back of another and pulls the robe off the hanged man.*) And now (*to* **The Nephew**) you be off so that we can put the right arse on the right seat. (*To* **Azdak**:) Step forward, you, and sit on the Judge's seat. (**Azdak** *hesitates.*) Sit down up there, man. (**Azdak** *is thrust on to the seat by the Ironshirts.*) The Judge was always a rascal. Now the rascal shall be the Judge. (*The Judge's robe is placed round his shoulders, the wicker from a bottle on his head.*) Look! There's a Judge for you!

The Singer

Now there was civil war in the land. The rulers were unsafe.
Now Azdak was made a Judge by the Ironshirts.
Now Azdak remained a Judge for two years.

The Singer With His Musicians

Great houses turn to ashes
 And blood runs down the street.
Rats come out of the sewers
 And maggots out of the meat.
The thug and the blasphemer
 Lounge by the altar-stone:
Now, now, now Azdak
 Sits on the Judgment throne.

Azdak *sits on the Judge's seat peeling an apple.* **Shauva** *sweeps out the hall. On one side an invalid in a wheelchair, the accused doctor and a man in rags with a limp; opposite, a young man accused of blackmail. An Ironshirt stands on guard holding the Ironshirts' banner.*

Azdak In view of the large number of cases, the Court today will hear two cases simultaneously. Before I open the proceedings, a short announcement: I receive (*he stretches out his hand; only* **The Blackmailer** *produces some money and hands it to him*) I reserve for myself the right to punish one of these parties here (*he glances *at* **The Invalid**) for contempt of court. You (*to* **The Doctor**) are a doctor, and you (*to* **The Invalid**) are bringing a complaint against him. Is the doctor responsible for your condition?

The Invalid Yes. I had a stroke because of him.

Azdak That sounds like professional negligence.

The Invalid More than negligence. I gave this man money to study. So far he hasn't paid me back one penny. And when I heard he was treating a patient free, I had a stroke.

Azdak Rightly. (*To* **The Limping Man**.) And you, what do you want here?

The Limping Man I'm the patient, your Worship.

Azdak He treated your leg?

The Limping Man Not the right one. My rheumatism was in the left leg, and he operated on my right. That's why I'm limping now.

Azdak And you got that free?

The Invalid A 500-piastre operation free! For nothing! For a God-Bless-You! And I paid this man's studies! (*To* **The Doctor**:) Did you learn to operate for nothing at school?

The Doctor (*to* **Azdak**) Your Worship, it is actually the custom to demand the fee before the operation, as the patient is more willing to pay before an operation than after. Which is only human. In this case I was convinced, when I started the operation, that my servant had already received the fee. In this I was mistaken.

The Invalid He was mistaken! A good doctor doesn't make mistakes. He examines before he operates.

Azdak That's right. (*To* **Shauva**:) Public Prosecutor, what's the other case about?

Shauva (*busily sweeping*) Blackmail.

The Blackmailer High Court of Justice, I'm innocent. I only wanted to find out from the landowner in question if he really had raped his niece. He kindly informed me that this was not the case, and gave me the money only so that I could let my uncle study music.

Azdak Ah ha! (*To* **The Doctor**:) You on the other hand can't produce any extenuating circumstances in your defence?

The Doctor Except that to err is human.

Azdak And you know that in money matters a good doctor is conscious of his responsibility? I once heard of a doctor who made a thousand piastres out of one sprained finger: he discovered it had something to do with the circulation of the blood, which a less good doctor would have overlooked. On another occasion, by careful treatment, he turned a mediocre gall bladder into a gold mine. You have no excuse, Doctor. The corn merchant Uxu made his son study medicine to get some knowledge of trade – our medical schools are that good. (*To* **The Blackmailer**:) What's the name of the landowner?

Shauva He doesn't want it to be known.

Azdak In that case I will pass judgment. The Court considers the blackmail proved. And you (*to* **The Invalid**) are sentenced to a fine of 1,000 piastres. If you get a second stroke the doctor will have to treat you free and if necessary amputate. (*To* **The Limping Man**:) As compensation, you will receive a bottle of embrocation. (*To* **The Blackmailer**:) You are sentenced to hand over half the proceeds of your deal to the Public Prosecutor, to keep the landowner's name secret. You are advised, moreover, to study medicine. You seem well suited to that profession. And you, Doctor, are acquitted because of an inexcusable professional mistake. The next cases!

The Singer With His Musicians
Beware of willing Judges
For Truth is a black cat
In a windowless room at midnight
And Justice a blind bat.
A third and shrugging party
Alone can right our wrong.

This, this, this, Azdak
Does for a mere song.

Enter **Azdak** *from the caravansary on the highway, followed by the old, bearded innkeeper. The Judge's seat is carried by a manservant and* **Shauva**. *An Ironshirt with a banner takes up position.*

Azdak Put it here. Then at least we can get some air and a little breeze from the lemon grove over there. It's good for Justice to do it in the open. The wind blows her skirts up and you can see what's underneath. Shauva, we have eaten too much. These rounds of inspection are very exhausting. (*To* **The Innkeeper**:) So it's about your daughter-in-law?

The Innkeeper Your Worship, it's about the family honour. I wish to bring an action on behalf of my son, who's gone on business across the mountain. This is the offending stableman, and here's my unfortunate daughter-in-law. (*Enter the daughter-in-law, a voluptuous wench. She is veiled.*)

Azdak (*sitting down*) I receive. (*Sighing,* **The Innkeeper** *hands him some money.*) Good. Now the formalities are disposed of. This is a case of rape?

The Innkeeper Your Worship, I surprised this rascal in the stable in the act of laying our Ludovica in the straw.

Azdak Quite right, the stable. Beautiful horses. I particularly like the little roan.

The Innkeeper The first thing I did of course was to berate Ludovica on behalf of my son.

Azdak (*seriously*) I said I liked the little roan.

The Innkeeper (*coldly*) Really? – Ludovica admitted that the stableman took her against her will.

Azdak Take off your veil, Ludovica. (*She does so.*) Ludovica, you please the Court. Tell us how it happened.

Ludovica (*as though well rehearsed*) When I entered the stable to look at the new foal, the stableman said to me of his own accord:

'It's hot today' and laid his hand on my left breast. I said to him: 'Don't do that!' But he continued to handle me indecently, which provoked my anger. Before I realized his sinful intentions, he became intimate with me. It had already happened when my father-in-law entered and accidentally trod on me.

The Innkeeper (*explaining*) On behalf of my son.

Azdak (*to* **The Stableman**) Do you admit that you started it?

The Stableman Yes.

Azdak Ludovica, do you like to eat sweet things?

Ludovica Yes, sunflower seeds.

Azdak Do you like sitting a long time in the tub?

Ludovica Half an hour or so.

Azdak Public Prosecutor, just drop your knife on the floor. (**Shauva** *does so.*) Ludovica, go and pick up the Public Prosecutor's knife.

Ludovica, *hips swaying, goes and picks up the knife.*

Azdak (*points at her*) Do you see that? The way it sways? The criminal element has been discovered. The rape has been proved. By eating too much, especially sweet things, by lying too long in warm water, by laziness and too soft a skin, you have raped the poor man. Do you imagine you can go around with a bottom like that and get away with it in Court? This is a case of deliberate assault with a dangerous weapon. You are sentenced to hand over to the Court the little roan which your father liked to ride on behalf of his son. And now, Ludovica, come with me to the stable so that the Court may investigage the scene of the crime.

Azdak *is carried on his Judge's seat by Ironshirts from place to place on the Grusinian highway. Behind him come* **Shauva** *dragging the gallows and* **The Stableman** *leading the little roan.*

The Singer With His Musicians

No more did the Lower Orders
    Tremble in their shoes

At the bellows of their Betters
  At Come-Here's and *Listen-You*'s.
His balances were crooked
  But they shouted in the streets: –
'Good, good, good is Azdak
  And the measure that he metes!'

He took them from Wealthy Peter
  To give to Penniless Paul
Sealed his illegal judgments
  With a waxen tear, and all
The rag-tag-and-bobtail
  Ran crying up and down: –
'Cheer, cheer, cheer for Azdak
  The darling of the town!'

The little group slowly withdraws.

To love your next-door neighbour
  Approach him with an axe
For prayers and saws and sermons
  Are unconvincing facts.
What miracles of preaching
  A good sharp blade can do:
So, so, so, so Azdak
  Makes miracles come true.

Azdak*'s Judge's seat is in a tavern. Three farmers stand before* **Azdak**. **Shauva** *brings him wine. In a corner stands an old peasant woman. In the open doorway, and outside, stand villagers and spectators. An Ironshirt stands guard with a banner.*

Azdak The Public Prosecutor opens the proceedings.

Shauva It's about a cow. For five weeks the defendant has had a cow in her stable, the property of farmer Suru. She was also found to be in the possession of a stolen ham. And cows belonging to farmer Shutoff were killed after he had asked the defendant to pay the rent for a field.

The Farmers It's about my ham, Your Worship. – It's about my cow, Your Worship. – It's about my field, Your Worship.

Azdak Granny, what have you got to say to all this?

The Old Woman Your Worship, one night towards morning, five weeks ago, there was a knock at my door, and outside stood a bearded man with a cow. He said, 'Dear woman, I am the miracle-working St Banditus. And because your son has been killed in the war, I bring you this cow as a keepsake. Take good care of it!'

The Farmers The robber Irakli, Your Worship! – Her brother-in-law, Your Worship! The cattle thief, the incendiary! – He must be beheaded!

Outside a woman screams. The crowd grows restless and retreats. Enter **The Bandit** *Irakli, with a huge axe.*

The Farmers Irakli! *They cross themselves.*

The Bandit A very good evening, dear friends! A glass of wine!

Azdak Public Prosecutor, a jug of wine for the guest. And who are you?

The Bandit I'm a wandering hermit, Your Worship. And thank you for the kind gift. (*He empties the glass which* **Shauva** *has brought.*) Same again!

Azdak I'm Azdak. (*He gets up and bows.* **The Bandit** *also bows.*) The Court welcomes the stranger hermit. Go on with your story, Granny.

The Old Woman Your Worship, that first night I didn't know that St Banditus could work miracles, it was only the cow. But one night a few days later the farmer's servants came to take the cow away from me. Then they turned round in front of my door and went off without the cow. And on their heads sprouted bumps big as a fist. Then I knew that St Banditus had changed their hearts and turned them into friendly people.

The Bandit *roars with laughter.*

The First Farmer I know what changed them.

Azdak That's good. You can tell us later. Continue.

The Old Woman Your Worship, the next one to become a good man was farmer Shutoff – a devil, as everyone knows. But St Banditus brought it about that Shutoff let me off paying the rent for the field.

The Second Farmer Because my cows were killed in the field.

The Bandit *laughs.*

The Old Woman (*answering* **Azdak***'s sign to continue*) And then one morning the ham came flying in at my window. It hit me in the small of the back. I've been lame ever since. Look, Your Worship. (*She limps a few steps.* **The Bandit** *laughs.*) I ask Your Worship: when was a poor old body ever given a ham except by a miracle?

The Bandit *starts sobbing.*

Azdak (*rising from his seat*) Granny, that's a question that strikes straight at the Court's heart. Be so kind as to sit down here.

Hesitating, the old woman sits on the Judge's seat. **Azdak** *sits on the floor, glass in hand.*

Little mother, I almost called you Mother Grusinia, the
woebegone
The bereaved one, whose sons are in the war.
Who is beaten with fists, but full of hope.
Who weeps when she is given a cow
And is surprised when she is not beaten.
Little mother, pass merciful sentence on us, the damned!

He bellows to **The Farmers**.

Admit that you don't believe in miracles, you atheists! Each of you is sentenced to pay 500 piastres! For your lack of faith. Get out!

The Farmers *creep out.*

And you, little mother, and you (*to* **The Bandit**) pious man, drink a jug of wine with the Public Prosecutor and Azdak!

The Singer with his Musicians
To feed the starving people
He broke the laws like bread

There on the seat of justice
  With the gallows over his head
For more than seven hundred
  Days he calmed their wails
Well, well, well, did Azdak
  Measure with false scales.

Two summers and two winters
  A poor man judged the poor
And on the wreck of justice
  He brought them safe to shore
For he spoke in the mob language
  That the mob understands.
I, I, I, cried Azdak
  Take bribes from empty hands.

The Singer

Then the era of disorder was over, the Grand Duke returned
The Governor's wife returned, a Judgment was held.
Many people died, the suburbs burned anew, and fear seized
  Azdak.

Azdak's *Judge's seat stands again in the Court of Justice.* **Azdak** *sits on the ground mending a shoe and talking to* **Shauva**. *Noises outside. Above a wall the fat prince's head is carried by on a lance.*

Azdak Shauva, your days of slavery are numbered, perhaps even the minutes. For a long time I have held you on the iron curb of reason, and it has made your mouth bloody. I have lashed you with arguments founded on reason, and ill-treated you with logic. You are by nature a weak creature, and if one slyly throws you an argument, you have to devour it; you can't resist. By nature you are compelled to lick the hand of a superior being, but superior beings can be very different. And now comes your liberation, and you will soon be able to follow your inclinations, which are low. You will be able to follow your unerring instinct, which teaches you to plant your heavy boot on the faces of men. Gone is the era of confusion and disorder, and the great times which I found described in the

Song of Chaos have not yet come. Let us now sing that song together in memory of those wonderful days. Sit down and don't violate the music. Don't be afraid. It sounds all right. It has a popular refrain.

He sings.

Sister, hide your face; brother, take your knife, the times are out of joint.
The noblemen are full of complaints, the simple folk full of joy.
The city says: let us drive the strong ones out of our midst.
Storm the government buildings, destroy the lists of the serfs.
Now the masters' noses are put to the grindstone. Those who never saw the day have emerged.
The poor-boxes of ebony are broken, the precious sesame wood is used for beds.
He who lacked bread now possesses barns; he who lived on the corn of charity, now measures it out himself.

Shauva Oh, oh, oh, oh.

Azdak

Where are you, General? Please, please, please, restore order.
The son of the nobleman can no longer be recognized; the child of the mistress becomes the son of her slave.
The councillors are taking shelter in the barn; he who was barely allowed to sleep on the wall now lolls in bed.
He who once rowed a boat now owns ships; when their owner looks for them, they are no longer his.
Five men are sent out by their master. They say: go yourself, we have arrived.

Shauva Oh, oh, oh, oh.

Azdak

Where are you, General? Please, please, please restore order!

Yes, so it might have been, if order had been much longer neglected. But now the Grand Duke, whose life I saved like a fool, has returned to the Capital. And the Persians have lent him an army to restore order. The outer town is already in flames. Go and get me the Big Book I like to sit on. (**Shauva** *brings the book from the*

Judge's seat. **Azdak** *opens it.*) This is the Statute Book and I've always used it, as you can confirm.

Shauva Yes, to sit on.

Azdak Now I'd better look and see what they can do to me, because I've always allowed the have-nots to get away with everything. And I'll have to pay for it dearly. I helped to put Poverty on to its rickety legs, so they'll hang me for drunkenness. I peeped into the rich man's pocket, which is considered bad taste. And I can't hide anywhere, for all the world knows me, since I have helped the world.

Shauva Someone's coming!

Azdak (*in a panic walks trembling to the seat*) The game is up! But I'll give no man the pleasure of seeing human greatness. I'll beg on my knees for mercy. Spittle will slobber down my chin. The fear of death is upon me.

Enter Natella Abashvili, **The Governor's Wife**, *followed by the Adjutant and an Ironshirt.*

The Governor's Wife What kind of man is that, Shalva?

Azdak A willing one, Your Excellency, a man ready to oblige.

The Adjutant Natella Abashvili, wife of the late Governor, has just returned and is looking for her three-year-old son, Michael. She has been informed that the child was abducted to the mountains by a former servant.

Azdak It will be brought back, Your Highness, at your service.

The Adjutant They say that the person in question is passing it off as her own child.

Azdak She will be beheaded, Your Highness, at your service.

The Adjutant That's all.

The Governor's Wife (*leaving*) I don't like that man.

Azdak (*following her to the door, and bowing*) Everything will be arranged, Your Highness, at your service.

Scene Six: The Chalk Circle

The Singer

Now listen to the story of the trial concerning the child of the
Governor Abashvili
To establish the true mother
By the famous test of the Chalk Circle.

The courtyard of the lawcourts in Nukha. Ironshirts lead Michael in, then go across the stage and out at the back. One Ironshirt holds **Grusha** *back under the doorway with his lance until the child has been taken away. Then she is admitted. She is accompanied by the former* **Governor***'s cook. Distant noises and a fire-red sky.*

Grusha He's so good, he can wash himself already.

The Cook You're lucky. This is not a real Judge; this is Azdak. He's a drunk and doesn't understand anything. And the biggest thieves have been acquitted by him, because he mixes everything up and because the rich never offer him big enough bribes. The likes of us get off lightly sometimes.

Grusha I need some luck today.

The Cook Touch wood. (*She crosses herself.*) I think I'd better say a quick prayer that the Judge will be drunk.

Her lips move in prayer, while **Grusha** *looks round in vain for the child.*

The Cook What I can't understand is why you want to hold on to it at any price, if it's not yours. In these days.

Grusha It's mine, I've brought it up.

The Cook But didn't you ever wonder what would happen when she returned?

Grusha At first I thought I'd give it back to her. Then I thought she wouldn't return.

The Cook And a borrowed coat keeps one warm, too, eh? (**Grusha** *nods.*) I'll swear anything you like, because you're a decent person. (*Memorizes aloud:*) I had him in my care for five piastres, and on Thursday evening, when the riots started, Grusha came to fetch him. (*She sees the soldier, Chachava, approaching.*) But you have done Simon great wrong. I've talked to him. He can't understand it.

Grusha (*unaware of* **Simon**'*s presence*) I can't be bothered with that man just now, if he doesn't understand anything.

The Cook He has understood that the child is not yours; but that you're married and won't be free until death parts you – he can't understand that.

Grusha *sees* **Simon** *and greets him.*

Simon (*gloomily*) I wanted to tell the woman that I am ready to swear I am the father of the child.

Grusha (*low*) That's right, Simon.

Simon At the same time, I would like to say that I am hereby not bound to anything; nor the woman, either.

The Cook That's unnecessary. She's married. You know that.

Simon That's her business and doesn't need rubbing in.

Enter two Ironshirts.

The Ironshirts Where's the Judge? – Has anyone seen the Judge?

Grusha (*who has turned away and covered her face*) Stand in front of me. I shouldn't have come to Nukha. If I run into the Ironshirt, the one I hit over the head . . .

The Ironshirt who has brought in the child steps forward.

The Ironshirt The Judge isn't here.

The two Ironshirts go on searching.

The Cook I hope something hasn't happened to him. With any other Judge you'd have less chance than a chicken has teeth.

Enter another Ironshirt.

The Ironshirt (*who had inquired for the Judge, to* **The Other Ironshirt**) There are only two old people and a child here. The Judge has bolted.

The Other Ironshirt Go on searching!

The first two Ironshirts exit quickly. The third remains behind. **Grusha** *lets out a scream. The Ironshirt turns round. He is* **The Corporal**, *and has a large scar right across his face.*

The Ironshirt (*in the gateway*) What's the matter, Shotta? Do you know her?

The Corporal (*after a long stare*) No.

The Ironshirt She's the one who's supposed to have stolen the Abashvili child. If you know anything about it, Shotta, you can make a packet of money.

Exit **The Corporal**, *cursing.*

The Cook Was it him? (**Grusha** *nods.*) I think he'll keep his mouth shut, otherwise he'll have to admit he was after the child.

Grusha (*relieved*) I'd almost forgotten I'd saved the child from them . . .

Enter **The Governor's Wife**, *followed by the Adjutant and two lawyers.*

The Governor's Wife Thank God! At least the common people aren't here. I can't stand their smell, it always gives me migraine.

The First Lawyer Madam, I must ask you to be as careful as possible in everything you say, until we have another Judge.

The Governor's Wife But I didn't say anything, Illo Shuboladze. I love the people – with their simple, straightforward ways. It's just their smell that brings on my migraine.

The Second Lawyer There will hardly be any spectators. Most of the population is behind locked doors because of the riots in the outer town.

The Governor's Wife (*looking at* **Grusha**) Is that the creature?

The First Lawyer I beg you, most gracious Natella Abashvili, to abstain from all invective until it is absolutely certain that the Grand Duke has appointed a new Judge and we have got rid of the present one, who is about the lowest ever seen in a Judge's robe. And things seem to be on the move, as you will see.

Ironshirts enter the courtyard.

The Cook Her Ladyship wouldn't hesitate to pull your hair out if she didn't know that Azdak is for the poor people. He goes by the face.

Two Ironshirts *begin by fastening a rope to the pillar.* **Azdak**, *in chains, is led in, followed by* **Shauva**, *also in chains. The three farmers bring up the rear.*

One Ironshirt Trying to run away, eh? (*He beats* **Azdak**.)

One Farmer Pull the Judge's robe off before we string him up!

Ironshirts and farmers pull the robe off **Azdak**. *His torn underwear becomes visible. Then someone kicks him.*

An Ironshirt (*pushing him on to someone else*) Anyone want a bundle of Justice? Here it is!

Accompanied by shouts of 'It's all yours!' and 'I don't want it!' they hurl **Azdak** *back and forth until he collapses. Then he is hauled up and dragged under the noose.*

The Governor's Wife (*who, during the 'ball-game', has been clapping her hands hysterically*) I disliked that man from the moment I first saw him.

Azdak (*covered in blood, panting*) I can't see. Give me a rag.

The Other Ironshirt What is it you want to see?

Azdak You, you dogs! (*He wipes the blood out of his eyes with his shirt.*) Good morning, dogs! How are you, dogs? How's the dog world? Does it stink good? Have you got another boot to lick? Are you back at each other's throats, dogs?

Enter a dust-covered rider accompanied by a corporal. He takes some documents from a leather case and looks through them. He interrupts.

The Rider Stop! I bring a despatch from the Grand Duke, containing the latest appointments.

The Corporal (*bellows*) Atten – shun!

All jump to attention.

The Rider Of the new Judge it says: We appoint a man whom we have to thank for the saving of a life of the utmost importance to the country. A certain Azdak in Nukha. Which is he?

Shauva (*pointing*) That's him on the gallows, Your Excellency.

The Corporal (*bellowing*) What's going on here?

The Ironshirt I ask to be allowed to report that His Worship has already been His Worship. He was declared the enemy of the Grand Duke only on these farmers' denunciation.

The Corporal (*pointing at* **The Farmers**) March them off! (*They are marched off, bowing incessantly.*) See to it that His Worship is exposed to no more indignities.

Exit **The Rider** *with* **The Corporal**.

The Cook (*to* **Shauva**) She clapped her hands! I hope he saw it!

The First Lawyer This is a catastrophe.

Azdak *has fainted. Coming to, he is dressed again in a Judge's robe. He walks away, swaying, from the group of Ironshirts.*

The Ironshirts Don't take it amiss, Your Worship. What are Your Worship's wishes?

Azdak Nothing, fellow dogs. An occasional boot to lick. (*To* **Shauva**.) I pardon you. (*He is unchained.*) Fetch me some of the red wine. The sweetest. (*Exit* **Shauva**.) Get out of here, I've got to judge a case. (*The Ironshirts go.* **Shauva** *returns with a jug of* *wine.* **Azdak** *takes deep gulps.*) Get me something for my backside. (**Shauva** *brings the Statute Book and puts it on the Judge's seat.* **Azdak** *sits on it.*) I receive! (*The faces of the prosecutors, among whom a worried council has been held, show smiles of relief. They whisper.*)

The Cook Oh dear!

Simon 'A well can't be filled with dew!' they say.

The Lawyers (*approaching* **Azdak**, *who stands up expectantly*) An absolutely ridiculous case, Your Worship. The accused has abducted the child and refuses to hand it over.

Azdak (*stretching out his hand, and glancing at* **Grusha**) A most attractive person. (*He receives more money.*) I open the proceedings and demand the absolute truth. (*To* **Grusha**:) Especially from you.

The First Lawyer High Court of Justice! Blood, as the saying goes, is thicker than water. This old proverb . . .

Azdak The Court wants to know the lawyer's fee.

The First Lawyer (*surprised*) I beg your pardon? (**Azdak** *rubs his thumb and index finger.*) Oh, I see. 500 piastres, Your Worship, is the answer to the Court's somewhat unusual question.

Azdak Did you hear? The question is unusual. I ask it because I listen to you in a quite different way if I know you are good.

The First Lawyer (*bowing*) Thank you, Your Worship. High Court of Justice! Of all bonds the bonds of blood are the strongest. Mother and child – is there a more intimate relationship? Can one tear a child from its mother? High Court of Justice! She has conceived it in the holy ecstasies of love. She has carried it in her womb. She has fed it with her blood. She has borne it with pain. High Court of Justice! It has been observed, Your Worship, how even the wild tigress, robbed of her young, roams restless through the mountains, reduced to a shadow. Nature herself . . .

Azdak (*interrupting, to* **Grusha**) What's your answer to all this and anything else the lawyer might have to say?

Grusha He's mine.

Azdak Is that all? I hope you can prove it. In any case, I advise you to tell me why you think the child should be given to you.

Grusha I've brought him up according to my best knowledge and conscience. I always found him something to eat. Most of the time he had a roof over his head. And I went to all sorts of trouble for him. I had expenses, too. I didn't think of my own comfort. I brought up the child to be friendly with everyone. And from the beginning I taught him to work as well as he could. But he's still very small.

The First Lawyer Your Worship, it is significant that the person herself doesn't claim any bond of blood between herself and this child.

Azdak The Court takes note.

The First Lawyer Thank you, Your Worship. Please permit a woman who has suffered much – who has already lost her husband and now also has to fear the loss of her child – to address a few words to you. Her Highness, Natella Abashvili . . .

The Governor's Wife (*quietly*) A most cruel fate, sir, forces me to ask you to return my beloved child. It's not for me to describe to you the tortures of a bereaved mother's soul, the anxiety, the sleepless nights, the . . .

The Second Lawyer (*exploding*) It's outrageous the way this woman is treated. She's not allowed to enter her husband's palace. The revenue of her estates is blocked. She is told cold-bloodedly that it's tied to the heir. She can't do anything without the child. She can't even pay her lawyers. (*To* **The First Lawyer** *who, desperate about this out-burst, makes frantic gestures to stop him speaking:*) Dear Illo Shuboladze, why shouldn't it be divulged now that it's the Abashvili estates that are at stake?

The First Lawyer Please, Honoured Sandro Oboladze! We had agreed . . . (*To* **Azdak***:*) Of course it is correct that the trial will also decide whether our noble client will obtain the right to dispose of the large Abashvili estates. I say 'also' on purpose, because in the foreground stands the human tragedy of a mother, as Natella

Abashvili has rightly explained at the beginning of her moving statement. Even if Michael Abashvili were *not* the heir to the estates, he would still be the dearly beloved child of my client.

Azdak Stop! The Court is touched by the mention of the estates. It's a proof of human feeling.

The Second Lawyer Thanks, Your Worship. Dear Illo Shuboladze, in any case we can prove that the person who took possession of the child is not the child's mother. Permit me to lay before the Court the bare facts. By an unfortunate chain of circumstances, the child, Michael Abashvili, was left behind while his mother was making her escape. Grusha, the Palace kitchenmaid, was present on this Easter Sunday and was observed busying herself with the child . . .

The Cook All her mistress was thinking about was what kind of dresses she would take along.

The Second Lawyer (*unmoved*) Almost a year later Grusha turned up in a mountain village with a child, and there entered into matrimony with . . .

Azdak How did you get into that mountain village?

Grusha On foot, Your Worship. And he was mine.

Simon I am the father, Your Worship.

The Cook I had him in my care for five piastres, Your Worship.

The Second Lawyer This man is engaged to Grusha, High Court of Justice, and for this reason his testimony is not reliable.

Azdak Are you the man she married in the mountain village?

Simon No, Your Worship, she married a peasant.

Azdak (*winking at* **Grusha**) Why? (*Pointing at* **Simon**.) Isn't he any good in bed? Tell the truth.

Grusha We didn't get that far. I married because of the child, so that he should have a roof over his head. (*Pointing at* **Simon**.) He was in the war, Your Worship.

Azdak And now he wants you again, eh?

Simon I want to state in evidence . . .

Grusha (*angrily*) I am no longer free, Your Worship.

Azdak And the child, you claim, is the result of whoring? (**Grusha** *does not answer.*) I'm going to ask you a question: What kind of child is it? Is it one of those ragged street-urchins? Or is it a child from a well-to-do family?

Grusha (*angrily*) It's an ordinary child.

Azdak I mean, did he have fine features from the beginning?

Grusha He had a nose in his face.

Azdak He had a nose in his face. I consider that answer of yours to be important. They say of me that once, before passing judgment, I went out and sniffed at a rosebush. Tricks of this kind are necessary nowadays. I'll cut things short now, and listen no longer to your lies. (*To* **Grusha**:) Especially yours. (*To the group of defendants:*) I can imagine what you've cooked up between you to cheat me. I know you. You're swindlers.

Grusha (*suddenly*) I can quite understand your wanting to cut it short, having seen what you received!

Azdak Shut up! Did I receive anything from you?

Grusha (*while the cook tries to restrain her*) Because I haven't got anything.

Azdak Quite true. I never get a thing from starvelings. I might just as well starve myself. You want justice, but do you want to pay for it? When you go to the butcher you know you have to pay. But to the Judge you go as though to a funeral supper.

Simon (*loudly*) 'When the horse was shod, the horsefly stretched out its leg', as the saying is.

Azdak (*eagerly accepting the challenge*) 'Better a treasure in the sewer than a stone in the mountain stream.'

Simon '"A fine day. Let's go fishing," said the angler to the worm.'

Azdak '"I'm my own master," said the servant, and cut off his foot.'

Simon '"I love you like a father," said the Czar to the peasant, and had the Czarevitch's head chopped off.'

Azdak 'The fool's worst enemy is himself.'

Simon But 'a fart has no nose'.

Azdak Fined ten piastres for indecent language in Court. That'll teach you what Justice is.

Grusha That's a fine kind of Justice. You jump on us because we don't talk so refined as that lot with their lawyers.

Azdak Exactly. The likes of you are too stupid. It's only right that you should get it in the neck.

Grusha Because you want to pass the child on to her. She who is too refined even to know how to change its nappies! You don't know any more about Justice than I do, that's clear.

Azdak There's something in that. I'm an ignorant man. I haven't even a decent pair of trousers under my robe. See for yourself. With me, everything goes on food and drink. I was educated in a convent school. Come to think of it, I'll fine you ten piastres, too. For contempt of Court. What's more, you're a very silly girl to turn me against you, instead of making eyes at me and wagging your backside a bit to keep me in a tood temper. Twenty piastres!

Grusha Even if it were thirty, I'd tell you what I think of your justice, you drunken onion! How dare you talk to me as though you were the cracked Isaiah on the church window! When they pulled you out of your mother, it wasn't planned that you'd rap her over the knuckles for pinching a little bowl of corn from somewhere! Aren't you ashamed of yourself when you see how afraid I am of you? But you've let yourself become their servant. So that their houses are not taken away, because they've stolen them. Since when do houses belong to bed-bugs? But you're on the look-out, otherwise they couldn't drag our men into their wars. You bribe-taker!

Azdak *gets up. He begins to beam. With a little hammer he knocks on the table half-heartedly as if to get silence. But as* **Grusha***'s scolding continues, he only beats time with it.*

I've no respect for you. No more than for a thief or a murderer with a knife, who does what he wants. You can take the child away from me, a hundred against one, but I tell you one thing: for a profession like yours, they ought to choose only bloodsuckers and men who rape children. As a punishment. To make them sit in judgment over their fellow men, which is worse than swinging from the gallows.

Azdak (*sitting down*) Now it will be thirty! And I won't go on brawling with you as though we were in a tavern. What would happen to my dignity as a Judge? I've lost all interest in your case. Where's the couple who wanted a divorce? (*To* **Shauva**.) Bring them in. This case is adjourned for fifteen minutes.

The First Lawyer (*to* **The Governor's Wife**) Without producing any more evidence, Madam, we have the verdict in the bag.

The Cook (*to* **Grusha**) You've gone and spoiled your chances with him. You won't get the child now.

Enter a very old couple.

The Governor's Wife Shalva, my smelling salts!

Azdak I receive. (*The old couple do not understand.*) I hear you want to be divorced. How long have you been living together?

The Old Woman Forty years, Your Worship.

Azdak And why d'you want a divorce?

The Old Man We don't like each other, Your Worship.

Azdak Since when?

The Old Woman Oh, from the very beginning, Your Worship.

Azdak I'll consider your case and deliver my verdict when I'm finished with the other one. (**Shauva** *leads them into the* *background.*) I need the child. (*He beckons* **Grusha** *towards him and bends not unkindly towards her.*) I've noticed that you have a soft spot for justice. I don't believe he's your child, but if he were yours, woman, wouldn't you want him to be rich? You'd only have to say he isn't yours and at once he'd have a palace, scores of horses in his stable, scores of beggars on his doorstep, scores of soldiers in his service, and scores of petitioners in his courtyard. Now, what d'you say? Don't you want him to be rich?

Grusha *is silent.*

The Singer Listen now to what the angry girl thought, but didn't say. (*He sings:*)

He who wears the shoes of gold
Tramples on the weak and old
Does evil all day long
And mocks at wrong.

O to carry as one's own
Heavy is the heart of stone.
The power to do ill
Wears out the will.

Hunger he will dread
Not those who go unfed:
Fear the fall of night
But not the light.

Azdak I think I understand you, woman.

Grusha I won't give him away. I've brought him up, and he knows me.

Enter **Shauva** *with the child.*

The Governor's Wife It's in rags!

Grusha That's not true. I wasn't given the time to put on his good shirt.

The Governor's Wife It's been in a pig-sty.

Grusha (*furious*) I'm no pig, but there are others who are. Where did you leave your child?

The Governor's Wife I'll let you have it, you vulgar person. (*She is about to throw herself on* **Grusha**, *but is restrained by her lawyers.*) She's a criminal! She must be flogged! Right away!

The Second Lawyer (*holding his hand over her mouth*) Most gracious Natella Abashvili, you promised . . . Your Worship, the plaintiff's nerves . . .

Azdak Plaintiff and defendant! The Court has listened to your case, and has come to no decision as to who the real mother of this child is. I as Judge have the duty of choosing a mother for the child. I'll make a test. Shauva, get a piece of chalk and draw a circle on the floor. (**Shauva** *does so.*) Now place the child in the centre. (**Shauva** *puts Michael, who smiles at* **Grusha**, *in the centre of the circle.*) Plaintiff and defendant, stand near the circle, both of you. (**The Governor's Wife** *and* **Grusha** *step up to the circle.*) Now each of you take the child by a hand. The true mother is she who has the strength to pull the child out of the circle, towards herself.

The Second Lawyer (*quickly*) High Court of Justice, I protest! I object that the fate of the great Abashvili estates, which are bound up with the child as the heir, should be made dependent on such a doubtful wrestling match. Moreover, my client does not command the same physical strength as this person, who is accustomed to physical work.

Azdak She looks pretty well fed to me. Pull!

The Governor's Wife *pulls the child out of the circle to her side.* **Grusha** *has let it go and stands aghast.*

The First Lawyer (*congratulating* **The Governor's Wife**) What did I say! The bonds of blood!

Azdak (*to* **Grusha**) What's the matter with you? You didn't pull!

Grusha I didn't hold on to him. (*She runs to* **Azdak**.) Your Worship, I take back everything I said against you. I ask your forgiveness. If I could just keep him until he can speak properly. He knows only a few words.

Azdak Don't influence the Court! I bet you know only twenty yourself. All right, I'll do the test once more, to make certain.

The two women take up positions again.

Azdak Pull!

Again **Grusha** *lets go of the child.*

Grusha (*in despair*) I've brought him up! Am I to tear him to pieces? I can't do it!

Azdak (*rising*) And in this manner the Court has established the true mother. (*To* **Grusha**:) Take your child and be off with it. I advise you not to stay in town with him. (*To* **The Governor's Wife**:) And you disappear before I fine you for fraud. Your estates fall to the city. A playground for children will be made out of them. They need one, and I have decided it shall be called after me – The Garden of Azdak.

The Governor's Wife *has fainted and is carried out by the Adjutant. Her lawyers have preceded her.* **Grusha** *stands motionless.* **Shauva** *leads the child towards her.*

Azdak Now I'll take off this Judge's robe – it has become too hot for me. I'm not cut out for a hero. But I invite you all to a little farewell dance, outside on the meadow. Oh, I had almost forgotten something in my excitement. I haven't signed the decree for divorce.

Using the Judge's seat as a table, he writes something on a piece of paper and prepares to leave. Dance music has started.

Shauva (*having read what is on the paper*) But that's not right. You haven't divorced the old couple. You've divorced Grusha from her husband.

Azdak Have I divorced the wrong ones? I'm sorry, but it'll have to stand. I never retract anything. If I did, there'd be no law and order. (*To the old couple:*) Instead, I'll invite you to my feast. You won't mind dancing with each other. (*To* **Grusha** *and* **Simon**:) I've still got 40 piastres coming from you.

Simon (*pulling out his purse*) That's cheap, Your Worship. And many thanks.

Azdak (*pocketing the money*) I'll need it.

Grusha So we'd better leave town tonight, eh, Michael? (*About to take the child on her back. To* **Simon**:) You like him?

Simon (*taking the child on his back*) With my respects, I like him.

Grusha And now I can tell you: I took him because on that Easter Sunday I got engaged to you. And so it is a child of love. Michael, let's dance.

She dances with Michael. **Simon** *dances with the cook. The old couple dance with each other.* **Azdak** *stands lost in thought. The dancers soon hide him from view. Occasionally he is seen again, but less and less as more couples enter and join the dance.*

The Singer

And after this evening Azdak disappeared and was never seen again.
But the people of Grusinia did not forget him and often remembered
His time of Judgment as a brief
Golden Age that was almost just.

The dancing couples dance out. **Azdak** *has disappeared.*

But you, who have listened to the story of the Chalk Circle
Take note of the meaning of the ancient song:
That what there is shall belong to those who are good for it, thus
The children to the maternal, that they thrive;
The carriages to good drivers, that they are driven well;
And the valley to the waterers, that it shall bear fruit.

Notes

Scene 1

28 *kolchos* – collective farm. Between 1929 and 1938 under Stalin land was taken out of the hands of individual peasants and merged into large holdings which could be worked collectively on a large scale. The system has not yet been able to feed the Russian people efficiently.

29 *Caucasian village* – the Caucasus is a range of mountains lying between the Black Sea and the Caspian Sea, covering an area historically fought over by Russia, Turkey and Iran. On its southern slopes lies the province of Georgia, which was occupied by the Red Army in 1921 and became a republic within the Soviet Union. Stalin was a Georgian. In the Second World War the Caucasus was the scene of heavy fighting from 1942 until the Germans were driven out in 1944.

29 *A Girl Tractor Driver* – the tractor driver who represents the mechanisation and modernisation of agriculture under Communism is something of a stock figure in Soviet-inspired works of Socialist Realism. That the driver is a girl here indicates the important role of women in building the new society.

29 *I set fire to it* – setting fire to all usable plant, buildings and crops ahead of the advancing Germans was a military tactic known as the scorched earth policy.

29 *Nukha* – an ancient city on the southern slopes of the Caucasus in eastern Georgia.

29 *Rosa Luxemburg* – (1870–1919) a German socialist of Polish extraction who was instrumental in founding the German Communist Party. She was murdered by right-wing para-militaries of the Freikorps in 1919. In 1934 a delegation of German writers visited a wine collective named after her near Tbilisi. They commented favourably on the international workforce of Russians, Turks and Germans, and on an ambitious irrigation scheme.

30 *why does one love one's country* – the Expert makes it clear that there is room in the system not only for the rational approach which is about to be stressed, but also for emotional ties to the land.

31 *but to Prince Kazbeki* – by the Russian Revolution; this implies that the old man was released from feudal bondage by the Revolution in 1917. An ancestor of Prince Kazbeki appears in Scenes 2 and 5 in the Chinese play.

31 *According to the law* – The concept of a law based not on precedent, or on established codes, but on constant reassessment of social desirability links *The Struggle for the Valley* with the ancient play that follows.

31 *a piece of land as a tool* – the Expert gives an elementary lesson on the socialist view of land. Not only is it not private property, it is not even the hereditary right of any group, but a national asset from which the community expects a return. It should therefore go to whoever can put it to most productive use. That Soviet agriculture would prove inefficient is something Brecht did not foresee, or even recognize when he saw it.

32 *without ammunition for our few rifles* – the fruit-growers had taken to the hills as partisans during the German occupation (1942–4). The reminder that the irrigation plan was conceived during the resistance disposes even the goat-breeders favourably towards it, as the applause all round shows.

32 *Mayakovsky* – Vladimir Mayakovsky (1893–1930), a Russian born in Georgia, was a poet and dramatist of the Revolution who, like Brecht, was accused of formalism under Stalin. He committed suicide in 1930 and had not been rehabilitated when Brecht used this quotation.

33 *machines and projects* – the constructive optimism with which Brecht invests Georgia in 1944 echoes the revolutionary pathos.

35 *old and new wisdom* – the old wisdom is the manner in which the Azdak resolves the conflict in *The Chalk Circle*, the new wisdom is the Soviet reason which has resolved the problem of the valley.

35 *Tiflis* – now Tbilisi, capital of Georgia.

Scene 2

35 *Once upon a time* – the Singer's ballad starts with the traditional fairy-tale formula and sets the scene for the Grusha episode.

35 *Grusinia* – from the German *Grusinien.* Brecht uses this old form which derives from the Russian for Georgia – Gruziya.

37 *Niko Mikadze* – and Mikha Loladze, the rival paediatricians, are a comic double act, down to their very names.

38 *The city lies still* – the Singer provides continuity, telling the audience that the next two figures they are going to meet are a kitchen maid

and a soldier. A bantering directness enters the dialogue when the lower-class figures appear. The tone is naive and flirtatious rather than earthy.

40 *Simon Chachava* – Grusha already knows his name.

40 *Not with another soldier!* – Brecht modulates the tone skilfully to show that the Soldier's intentions are serious, though his approach is playful.

40 *why are there armed men?* – the Singer's rhetorical questions complement the signs that pass between the Fat Prince and the Ironshirts, indicating economically that a palace revolution is afoot.

41 *not before the banquet* – this is the third time the Governor has refused to accept the rider's message, repetition making the significance of his non-speaking part clear.

41 *Chopped to pieces for the Governor* – dramatic irony, as the Ironshirt with the lance instantly proves.

42 *Oh, blindness of the great!* – there is an echo of Aeschylus as the Singer, like the chorus in Greek tragedy, pronounces moral judgement on the great. Brecht gives a Marxist twist to the baroque image of Fortune's wheel by making it the hope of the people – after the last revolution.

43 *share in their misfortunes* – the little people rarely share the good fortune – only the misfortunes – of the ruling classes. The divergent interests of the two classes which the Singer pinpoints here is a constant theme of Brecht's major plays, which sympathise with the oppressed class.

44 *How can stabbing harm the knife?* – by producing this piece of folk wisdom Simon Chachava prepares us for his proverb contest with Azdak later in the play.

44 *The soldier is a pig-headed man* – Grusha notices that Simon cannot see where his own interest lies. She will soon prove prone to the same error herself. 'The young lady' and 'the soldier' address one another in the third person to avoid sentimentality in the proposal scene.

46 *all is as it was* – having avoided sentiment in the previous dialogue, Brecht uses verse for Grusha's beautiful, comprehensive pledge. It is charged with dramatic irony since Grusha contracts (but does not consummate) a marriage in Simon's absence.

46 *harshly* – note the abrupt shifts of tone from one episode to the next.

50 *They'll slaughter whole families* – in a hereditary, dynastic society all possible successors have to be wiped out. The Czar's family were victims of this principle in Russia in 1917.

51 *stubbornly* – it is now Grusha's turn to ignore her own interests. There is an echo here of Kattrin in the officers' shirts scene in *Mother Courage* in the way Grusha gives in to her maternal instinct.

52 *The light grown dimmer* – in general, Brecht maintained an even, bright, white level of lighting, in keeping with the anti-illusionistic aims of his theatre. Here the dimmer is used to indicate the passage of time and is not intended as symbolic or atmospheric.

52 *Terrible is the temptation to do good!* – this paradox indicates that Grusha's humane gesture is going to cause her much trouble. The explanation is a social one; in an inhuman, exploitative society altruism is always a risk.

Scene 3

54 *A peasant's cottage appears* – in Brecht's own production the cottage travelled round to meet Grusha who was walking against the movement of the revolving stage.

54 *soldiers from the city* – the Ironshirts from Nukha have been plundering the countryside, causing shortages and forcing up prices.

55 *caravansary* – wayside inn or staging post for camel trains in the Middle East and Asia.

58 *Anastasia Katarinovska* – in an early version of the play Natella Abashvili was called Anastasia Abashvili, in which case it was clear that Grusha is posing as her former mistress in this scene.

58 *a look at your hands* – during the Russian Revolution, examination of the hands was a standard method of identifying non-proletarians; Brecht alluded to this in rehearsals of the play.

60 *Look before you leap* – the Servant, like Simon Chachava, has a predilection for proverbs. He is the first character to display class consciousness and solidarity with Grusha in her flight.

61 *a hollow reed or a tinkling cymbal* – This episode on the highway shows what Grusha is up against.

62 *You can't ask that of me, Michael* – Grusha has sized up the Peasant Woman and feels she is kind; she has milk and can provide for Michael, so Grusha can leave him with a clear conscience, aware that her own interests lie elsewhere.

64 *I always withdraw* – the Corporal puns on Grusha's words. The withdrawal he means is coitus interruptus. His speeches are sexually suggestive and full of menace.

65 *In this house* I *decide* – by making the wife act normally while the audience is aware of the approaching danger, Brecht builds up suspense.

Scene 4

73 *Has it got a father?* – Grusha shakes her head, meaning that the Governor is dead. Her brother assumes however that Michael is her illegitimate son and begins to think of a cover story for his pious wife.
74 *She has a good heart* – Lavrenti's word contrast with his wife's actions.
77 *A rubber stamp makes all the difference* – this is anachronistic, perhaps an ironic dig at German officialdom's obsession with rubber stamps, without which even the most trivial document is invalid.
77 *as a pear tree comes by the sparrows* – having agreed to the sham marriage, Grusha ruefully reflects that it was not in the first instance inclination, but the Puritan principle 'Waste not, want not' that led to her having Michael on her hands. The effect on her own life is now being brought home to her.
77 *A space divided by a partition* – the stage is split into two halves (see illustration). Thus the supposedly comatose husband can react to the wedding reception next door, and the audience sees all. A situation rich in comic possibilities.
78 *drying her tears* – the Mother-in-Law's respectability, like the Sister-in-Law's piety, is bogus, in this case a mere pretext for extorting another 200 piastres. Brecht wants to show a mercenary, capitalist society.
79 *in Latin* – the language of the Roman Catholic Church, not the vernacular of the people.
79 *Extreme Unction* – in the Catholic Church the sacrament administered to the dying.
81 *he charges a fortune* – the bourgeois professions, here the ministry, and later in the play medicine, are wholly mercenary.
82 *but against disorder* – though they are historic foes, their common class interest decrees that they close ranks when revolution threatens their status. Class consciousness outweighs patriotism.
82 *we'll have to pay for the war* – that wars are always fought at the people's expense is a theme that runs through Brecht's mature plays.
85 *It's against nature* – this indicates that the marriage has not been consummated.

85 *almanac* – a handbook of conventional wisdom.
86 *As the months passed by, the child grew up* – this poem in free rhythms evokes the passage of time and the fading of Simon's memory. It is his face Grusha sees in the water.
86 *Heads-off* – the game re-enacts the death of Michael's father. Michael wants a turn at beheading, but it must be done with a light touch so that Grusha's laughter makes sense, the laughter in turn is needed to make Simon's entrance effective.
87 *They found better fish than me* – Simon still inclines to speak in proverbs, or at least images. The conversation avoids the direct modes of address, I or you, and this keeps the emotional key low.
89 *it blows through every crack* – sexual innuendo. Simon believes the child is Grusha's.

Scene 5

91 *village clerk* – in these ancient times an educated man, and in Marxist categories a member of the intelligentsia. Drunk and in rags, Azdak is established right away as an eccentric, rebellious figure. In the Berliner Ensemble production Ernst Busch played both the Singer and Azdak. This has since become standard practice. Brecht's only comment is that Azdak must be played by the best *actor*, not the best singer.
91 *would go through the walls* – the stage directions show the Fugitive as a comic caricature of the helpless aristocrat, reduced by fear to a slobbering jelly in which it is impossible to recognise the Grand Murderer or Grand Thief of Azdak's later self-accusation (page 64).
91 *Grand Duke* – dramatic irony since, unbeknown to Adzak, it *is* the Grand Duke.
92 *Am hunted* – Brecht's German distinguishes the ruling classes by their clipped speech and short, incomplete sentences.
92 *Especially what they call weeds* – the curious logic of exterminating rabbits because they eat weeds, sets the comic note for Azdak's witty dumbfounding of the slow-witted Shauva.
93 *how a poor man behaves?* – Azdak shows how a poor man's table manners are conditioned by his social situation, and, demonstrates what Brecht means by 'gestus', the essential elements in a character's behaviour which the actor has to identify and reproduce if he is to get the social implications of his role across. The Fugitive gets a lesson in Brechtian acting.
94 *like Pontius Pilate into the Creed* – unintentionally and undeservedly.

94 *A new age has come* – Azdak has discovered that he has harboured the Grand Duke.

96 *Too long a war! And no justice!* – these are the two reasons Azdak gives for the Persian revolution. They apply equally to the October Revolution of 1917 in Russia, and they introduce the theme of disorder and justice which is central to the story of the judge.

96 *but the helmets have been paid for* – The song is a revolutionary indictment of the feudal system in both war and peace.

97 *our carpet weavers caught the 'Persian disease'* – referring to the revolution has failed. The beating 'to pulp for two piastres per weaver' echoes Great War atrocities when Austrian soldiers hanged Serbian dissidents for a few cigarettes a head. Azdak now grasps the situation.

98 *I let him escape?* – Azdak changes his tune, reminding the soldiers that he let the Grand Duke get away. He is no hero, and he is more concerned with survival than principles.

98 *burst out laughing* – They are content with a sadistic joke without actually harming Azdak physically.

100 *unmistakable gait of the Grand Duke* – the role Azdak is going to play is first introduced visually. He later mimics his speech mannerisms.

101 *From the point of view of taste, I mean* – Azdak as the Grand Duke has opened the proceedings in a tone of farce.

102 *howl like wolf* – the judge is a watchdog, the exploitative ruling classes the wolves.

102 *War lost only for Grusinia* – this is a constant theme in Brecht's mature plays. In war, the people always lose.

103 *The wicker from a bottle on his head* – again Brecht makes a visual point. The wicker hat makes a clown of the judge, keeping the element of farce to the fore.

103 *peeling an apple* – Brecht establishes the situation visually. Azdak disregards formality and eats an apple in the Judge's seat, which prepares the audience for his unconventional procedure.

107 *deliberate assault with a dangerous weapon* – the flourish with which Azdak pronounces the waggle of Ludovica's bottom to be criminal looks dangerously like male chauvinism, but Brecht sees her provocative appearance as a result of a life of bourgeois indolence and luxury. Her evidence sounds like a fabrication too.

112 *The Song of Chaos* – the narrator of the ballad is a nobleman, hence his appeal to the General to restore order. The song, which may be based on an ancient Egyptian original, is a catalogue of revolutionary

social change. Azdak observes that Grusinia's chance to reorganise society has passed.

113 *the have-nots to get away with everything* – Azdak assesses his own role as having been champion of the poor against the rich.

Scene 6

117 *lowest ever seen in the judge's robe* – the Cook and Grusha are hoping for Azdak with whom Grusha has a chance, but the Lawyers are hoping the restored Grand Duke will appoint a proper judge. From here Brecht keeps the outcome in the balance to the end.

118 *A certain Azdak in Nukha* – Brecht had used a despatch rider as *deus ex machina* once before, in *The Threepenny Opera.* By a miraculous coincidence the Grand Duke now appoints Azdak Judge as a reward for saving his life in Scene 5.

122 *a funeral supper* – a free meal.

123 *Czarevitch* – the eldest son of the Czar.

123 *But 'a fart has no nose'* – the corrupt cannot smell their own corruption.

124 *You bribe-taker!* – the irony here is that Grusha, with her first flood of eloquence in the play, expresses sentiments that are close to Azdak's own.

128 *the meaning of the ancient song* – Brecht brings the first and last scenes together, suggesting that the award of the child to the mother who has fostered him is analogous to the award of the valley to the fruit growers, which is now assumed to be the outcome of 'The Struggle for the Valley'. Both are rational decisions.